# AMERICA the BEAUTIFUL

# TEXAS

By R. Conrad Stein

**Consultants**

**Amy Jo Baker, Ed.D.,** Social Studies Curriculum Specialist, San Antonio Independent School District

**Christina B. Woll, M.A.,** Library Consultant, Palacios, Texas

**Marilyn von Kohl,** Director, Local Records Division, Texas State Library, Austin

**Robert L. Hillerich, Ph.D.,** Bowling Green State University, Bowling Green, Ohio

CHILDRENS PRESS®

CHICAGO

**Horses grazing near Amarillo**

Project Editor: Joan Downing
Associate Editor: Shari Joffe
Design Director: Margrit Fiddle
Typesetting: Graphic Connections, Inc.
Engraving: Liberty Photoengraving

Library of Congress Cataloging-in-Publication Data

Stein, R. Conrad.
    America the beautiful. Texas / by R. Conrad Stein.
        p.    cm.
    Includes index.
    Summary: Introduces the vast and diverse state with
deep historical roots in the lore of cowboys and oil
tycoons.
    ISBN 0-516-00489-1
    1.  Texas—Juvenile literature. [1.  Texas]  I.  Title.
F386.3.S73   1989                                88-38400
976.4—dc19                                        CIP
                                                  AC

976.4
S

The Houston
skyline from Sam
Houston Park

## TABLE OF CONTENTS

# Chapter 1

# THE TEXAS MYSTIQUE

# THE TEXAS MYSTIQUE

"I have said that Texas is a state of mind, but I think it is more than that. It is a mystique closely approximating a religion," claimed writer John Steinbeck. The dictionary defines the word *mystique* as "an attitude of mystical veneration conferred upon a person or thing." The Texas mystique is based on images that will never die.

To millions of people around the world, Texas is a place where brave but rootless cowboys ride the open range and where oil millionaires live in multimillion-dollar mansions. This impression, nurtured by movies and western novels, is far from reality. Today's Texans are equally likely to work as salespersons, machinists, and rocket scientists. Nevertheless, the lore of cowboys and oil tycoons has deep historical roots. The Texas cowboy era was one of the most exciting periods in American history, and during the state's oil booms, fortunes were made and lost in a matter of hours. The Texas mystique has been strengthened by its larger-than-life heroes such as Stephen Austin, Sam Houston, and Sam Rayburn. Indeed, the sheer size and variety of the state is legendary.

Texas is called the Lone Star State, a name that refers to the single star on the state flag, a reminder of its decade-long experience as a separate nation. Texas is also called, with great sincerity, the Friendship State. Texans welcome visitors with heartfelt warmth and graciousness. Texans are eager to talk about their state. Its history is more than just the story of a state—it is the saga of a vast and diverse empire.

# Chapter 2
# THE LAND

# THE LAND

An army private on leave once wrote to his fellow soldiers: "I am now about to travel from one end of the earth to the other—meaning I am going from East Texas to West Texas to visit my grandfather."

## GEOGRAPHY

Texas is a huge state, and its people love to boast about its tremendous size. For more than a century—until 1959 when Alaska entered the American Union—Texas was the largest state. Today's Texans delight in knowing that the states of New York, New Jersey, Ohio, Illinois, and Wisconsin could fit inside Texas's boundaries and still leave room to spare.

Texas forms a rough triangle along its southern border, and has a thick area shaped like a panhandle jutting up at the top.

Texas is located in the American Southwest. The state is bordered by Oklahoma on the north, and Arkansas and Louisiana on the east. The Gulf of Mexico forms the state's southeastern border, while the Rio Grande—separating the state from the Republic of Mexico—forms the southwestern border. Texas shares its western border with New Mexico.

## LAND FORMS

Texas is composed of four major land regions: the Gulf Coastal Plains, the North Central Plains, the Great Plains, and the Trans-Pecos Region.

Above: The Piney Woods, in
East Texas
Left: A ranch near La Grange,
in the Gulf Coastal Plains

The Gulf Coastal Plains, an immense lowland in the south and
east portion of Texas, covers about a third of the state. In the
easternmost reaches of the state, this region is characterized by a
belt of pine forests known as the Piney Woods. The Piney Woods
and the lands immediately to the west are suitable for diversified
farming and livestock raising. Expanses of rolling prairie in this
coastal plain were easily tilled, and supported the region's first
farming communities and earliest populations. The southern
sections of the Gulf Coastal Plains support irrigated and dry
farming; cotton and citrus fruits are among the notable crops.

At the west edge of the Gulf Coastal Plains stands a line of
southward and eastward facing hills. These balconylike hills,
called the Balcones Escarpment, mark the boundary between
lowland and upland Texas, the beginning of the North Central
Plains. The rolling prairies of the North Central Plains gradually
rise from about 750 feet (229 meters) to 2,500 feet (762 meters)
above sea level. Except along streams, the land is generally
treeless. There are some expanses of land suitable for cultivation,

**Horseback riders in Caprock Canyon State Park, in the Panhandle**

but most of the land is given over to the state's extensive cattle-raising industry.

The Great Plains of the Texas Panhandle are announced by the Cap Rock Escarpment. This natural rock boundary, formed by erosion, rises abruptly 200, 500, or in some places 1,000 feet (61, 152, or 305 meters) above the North Central Plains. North and west of the escarpment, the plains rise from 2,700 feet (823 meters) to 4,000 feet (1,219 meters) above sea level at the New Mexico border. Farming in this region depends on irrigation from underground water supplies. Some areas of the Great Plains offer grasses, weeds, and tree foliage suitable for cattle, sheep, and goats, respectively. The lands around the Colorado River contain a large number of minerals. In addition, the area, with ancient rocks near the earth's surface, is of great interest to geologists.

The Trans-Pecos Region (west of the Pecos River) is in the state's southwest corner. The region is rocky and water-starved, prompting an old Texas saying: "A jackrabbit has to graze at a lope here to keep from starving." Relatively recent discoveries of groundwater reserves have allowed much of this land to be irrigated to support cotton and alfalfa crops. The Trans-Pecos contains all of the state's mountains and its most haunting scenery, making it a popular tourist attraction.

Texts topography (clockwise from below):
The Chisos Mountains in Big Bend National Park;
the Rio Grande at St. Helena Canyon; Texas Hill Country;
gypsum dunes in Guadalupe Mountains National Park;
and the stark landscape of Enchanted Rock State Park

**The Rio Grande, which forms the border between Texas and Mexico, is the state's longest river.**

## RIVERS AND LAKES

A glance at a state map reveals a virtual spiderweb of rivers. The San Antonio, Colorado, Brazos, Trinity, and Neches are major rivers that flow southward to empty into the Gulf of Mexico. In the north, the Canadian River flows east across the Panhandle. Three rivers serve as state borderlines: the Sabine separates Texas from Louisiana, the Red River forms Oklahoma's border with Texas, and the Rio Grande forms the United States-Mexico border. In the western corner of the state, the Pecos is the Rio Grande's chief tributary.

Texas has hundreds of lakes, ranging from mere ponds to bodies of water so large that their shores stretch to the horizon. Many lakes were created when Texans dammed some of their rivers.

Unlike dams in other western states, only a few Texas dams are sources of hydroelectric power, as the rivers flow too slowly. However, the dams are a vital tool in water conservation, provide water for agricultural and industrial uses, and offer protection against flooding. Lake Texoma, created by a dam on the Red River, spreads into Oklahoma. Lake Meredith rests in the middle of the Panhandle, and Lake O' the Pines is a shining jewel in the Piney Woods. In spite of the number of lakes and rivers in the state, water is a precious, and sometimes scarce, natural resource. Many of the lakes were artificially created, many streams and rivers dry up for weeks at a time, and water evaporates quickly from shallow lakes during times of scant rainfall.

## THE COASTLINE

The Texas shore along the Gulf of Mexico stretches 367 miles (591 kilometers). Including bays, lagoons, and islands, Texas has more than 3,000 miles (4,828 kilometers) of coastal area. Much of the seashore consists of gentle beaches, as the land slips gently to the sea.

The Gulf Coast is home to many long, narrow barrier islands that serve as magnets for vacationers. The Padre Island National Seashore is one of the state's most popular attractions. No wonder, for during the summer months, the water surrounding the Padre Islands can become almost bathwater warm.

Texas's Gulf of Mexico coast includes several deep-water ports. Houston is the busiest of these, and in addition, is one of the chief cotton-shipping centers of the nation. Other large deep-water ports include Corpus Christi, Texas City, and Beaumont. The busy port city of Galveston is located on Galveston Island, just east of the mainland of Texas.

Among the most colorful plants that thrive in Texas are Indian paintbrush (top left) and Texas bluebonnets (top right), shown growing wild in a field near Brenham (top center). Purple sage (far right) and barrel cactus (right) also are common.

## PLANT AND ANIMAL LIFE

About 14 percent of Texas is forest-covered, with the densest woodlands standing in the well-watered east. Pines and oaks are the principal trees. In the drier western regions, mesquite trees, cactus, sagebrush, and chaparral grow. Nearly five hundred varieties of grasses can be found in the state, mostly in the prairies of the eastern and central regions. The most common include the bluestem, buffalo grass, and curly mesquite. Sideoats grama thrives in many of Texas's different soils and is the official state grass.

More than five thousand species of wildflowers—more varieties than are found in any other state—bloom in Texas. The land's

Wildlife found in Texas includes (clockwise from left) armadillos, pronghorn antelope, nearly extinct whooping cranes, white-tailed deer, and poisonous rattlesnakes.

great diversity, which ranges from sea level to mountains more than 8,000 feet (2,438 meters) high and from humid, near-tropical conditions to arid deserts, accounts for its amazing variety of flowers. Goldenrods, asters, daisies, sunflowers, and bluebonnets are among the most common varieties.

Many wildlife surveys give Texas the largest deer population of the fifty states. Pronghorn antelope, rabbits, foxes, raccoons, and bats are at home in Texas. The primitive-looking armadillo may be seen scurrying over the arid landscape. More than one hundred species of snakes live in Texas, including ten different kinds of poisonous rattlesnakes.

The climate at Palo Duro Canyon State Park, just south of Amarillo, is cool and dry because of the high altitude.

More than 550 species of birds—three-quarters of all the species identified in the United States—have been sighted in Texas. Among them are migratory birds such as ducks, geese, and egrets; game birds such as quail, wild turkeys, and doves; and predators such as owls, hawks, and southern bald eagles. Other birds of special interest include the roadrunner, the mockingbird, and the nearly extinct whooping crane and prairie chicken.

## CLIMATE

Because of Texas's immense size and the variety of landforms, the state's climate is diverse. For example, the Panhandle growing season is less than 200 days. In contrast, the Winter Garden area of the Rio Grande Valley has a growing season of 330 days. Temperatures in the Panhandle average 35 degrees Fahrenheit (1.6 degrees Celsius) in January and 79 degrees Fahrenheit (26 degrees Celsius) in July. The lower Rio Grande Valley's average temperatures are 60 degrees Fahrenheit (15.5 degrees Celsius) in January and 85 degrees Fahrenheit (29 degrees Celsius) in July. Snowfall, too, varies greatly from north to south: the Panhandle city of Amarillo has had snow every year since the 1880s;

Hurricanes along the Gulf Coast of Texas have caused havoc over the years. Galveston, hit by a hurricane in 1900 that killed 6,000 and destroyed the island, was in the path of Hurricane Alicia in 1983 (left). Twenty-one people were killed and damage was estimated at $2 billion.

Brownsville, the state's southernmost city, has not had a measurable snowfall during the twentieth century.

With few exceptions, the eastern region of the state receives greater rainfall than does the western. The Houston area averages about 45 inches (114 centimeters) of rain a year, while El Paso receives less than 10 inches (25.4 centimeters). In the Trans-Pecos Region, the word rain dominates conversations: "Did you get any? How much? Where?"

Texas weather is often unpredictable, and on rare occasions it is deadly. In 1987, a tornado ripped through the tiny West Texas town of Saragosa, killing 29 people. A powerful twister struck Wichita Falls in 1979, leaving 42 dead and 1,740 injured. Furious hurricanes sometimes sweep the Gulf Coast.

In 1900, a hurricane destroyed Galveston and killed 6,000 people. The Galveston tragedy remains the most deadly natural disaster in American history.

Although nature sometimes plays havoc with Texas, its citizens still revere the land. As one grizzled farmer put it, "It's a deceitful country. Hard. Mean. With floods and droughts and tornadoes. But look at it," said the old man as he swept his hand toward a tree-shaded riverbank. "God Almighty, it's so beautiful."

# Chapter 3
# THE PEOPLE

# THE PEOPLE

*Texas can be compared to a giant human magnet,*
*pulling in increasingly larger numbers of people.*
—The *Texas Almanac*

## POPULATION AND POPULATION DISTRIBUTION

The 1980 census counted 14,229,191 people living in Texas. This
figure makes Texas the country's third most-populous state. In
1960, it ranked sixth among the states. Then, during the 1970s, the
state's population grew by more than 3 million. Texas continued
to grow during the first half of the 1980s; its growth rate was
three times that of the national growth rate. This growth has been
recent—30 percent of the state's population has arrived since
1970, and there is every indication that this trend will continue.
Many forecasters predict that Texas will become the second most-
populous state before 1990. Migration from other states is the
primary reason behind Texas's rapid growth. People are attracted
by the eastern region's climate, and, despite an economic recession
in the late 1980s, the state's industries continue to attract job
seekers.

Even though the population has almost doubled since 1950,
Texas remains an uncrowded land. Its population density averages
54.3 persons per square mile (20.9 persons per square kilometer).
This is well below the national average of 64 persons per square
mile (24.7 persons per square kilometer). Again, Texas is so large
that one number cannot give an accurate picture. The eastern half

of the state, where many cities are located, has the greatest concentration of people. For instance, Dallas County, including parts of the city of Dallas, had a population density of 1,769 persons per square mile (683 persons per square kilometer) in 1980. The same year, Loving County had a population density of less than 1 person per square mile—in fact, there were fewer than 100 persons in the entire county!

In 1900, about 80 percent of Texans lived on farms, and only one city—San Antonio—had a population exceeding 50,000. Today, 80 percent of the people live in cities. In order of population, the state's largest cities are Houston, Dallas, San Antonio, El Paso, Fort Worth, Austin, and Corpus Christi.

## WHO ARE THE TEXANS?

For many centuries, several Indian groups lived in Texas. The Caddo farmed in the eastern regions, and the Apache and Comanche hunted in the high plains and plateaus of the west. The Tonkawa people lived in the central section of what is now Texas, and the Karankawa lived, primarily by fishing, along the Gulf Coast.

More than four hundred years ago, in 1541, Spanish explorers arrived in West Texas. The Spaniards had been exploring and colonizing the lands to the south of Texas. As they continued to rule and explore Mexico and the lands north of the Rio Grande River, many Spaniards married Indians native to Mexico. The people of mixed Spanish and Indian heritage were called *mestizos*. Some mestizos began to settle in Texas lands. From the late seventeenth century to the beginning of the nineteenth century, the mestizo people, moving northward from Mexico, were among the dominant settlers of Texas.

Among the early immigrants to Texas were Germans, who settled in the Fredericksburg area (left) in the 1800s. In recent years, the Asian population (above) has grown.

In the early nineteenth century, settlers from the eastern United States came to Texas. These were not white Americans (called Anglos), but Native Americans—Indians—who were being relocated because of the white settlers' desire for the Indians' eastern homelands. Among the Indian groups to resettle in Texas were the Cherokee, Alabama, Coushatta, Shawnee, Delaware, and Kickapoo. Claims of good, plentiful land brought white Americans from the southeastern United States. Many of these Anglos brought black slaves with them to labor on the farms they hoped to start. Some Anglos came to Texas not to farm or to ranch but to engage in money-making schemes that would help them regain lost fortunes. These entrepreneurs of yesterday were a driving force in the state's development. During the second half of the nineteenth century, Texas's reputation attracted immigrants directly from Europe. Germans led the way, followed by English, Irish, Scandinavians, Czechs, and Poles.

In the twentieth century, Texas again captured the imagination of people throughout North America. Many Mexicans have immigrated to the state, and in the last twenty years or so, many Americans have migrated to Texas from other states in the Union. Texas's history of migration and immigration has given the state a great tradition of ethnic diversity.

Today, about 66 percent of the state's people are white; Hispanics (almost all of whom are of Mexican origin) make up 21 percent; blacks comprise 12 percent; and other nonwhites make up about 1 percent. Texas is home to the nation's second-largest Hispanic population and the third-largest black population. Ninety-four percent of today's Texans were born in the United States. Asians are a fast-growing group, but represent less than 1 percent of the people.

## RELIGION AND LANGUAGE

Roman Catholics are the largest religious group in Texas. Baptists rank a close second. Other religious groups include Methodists, Episcopalians, members of the United Church of Christ, Jews, and Moslems.

Texans are often demonstrative in their religious activities. In many communities, Mexican Americans hold solemn processions to celebrate Easter, and joyous pageants to celebrate Christmas. Many of the state's Southern Baptists spend hours reading and holding animated discussions on the Bible.

English is the state's official language, but Spanish is spoken in most areas and it has a powerful impact in the south. Many Mexican Americans in South Texas conduct all their business in Spanish. Texas Anglos who live in the south usually know at least some Spanish. Most of the Texans whose ancestors immigrated to

25

Texas from Europe in the late 1800s no longer speak their Old World tongues. Those third- or fourth-generation Texans long ago traded in European dialects for the famous Texas drawl.

## REGIONALISM

Rarely does a Texan say merely "I'm from Texas." The statement just doesn't say enough. Texans look upon their state as a union of five regions: East Texas, West Texas, North Texas, Central Texas, and South Texas. Texas author and historian A.C. Greene points out: "People in other parts of the country often don't realize that when we say 'West Texas,' we capitalize the W. It's the same with all the other regions." These regions lack precise dividing lines, but the influence of regionalism is profound. Therefore, a true Texan is more likely to say, "I'm from West Texas," or "I'm from East Texas."

East Texas is the band of land that hugs the Louisiana border. It was settled, before the Civil War, by southerners who established a plantation system there. Many black Texans either live or have roots in East Texas. Much of the area is a place of small towns and a slow-paced, southern way of life.

The cities of Dallas and Fort Worth, as well as the sea of suburbs that surround them, form the nucleus of North Texas. Dallas and Fort Worth, only 33 miles (53 kilometers) apart, are often described as a single area called the "Metroplex." In the past, North Texans served as the merchants and storekeepers for the state. In fact, Dallas still leads the state in banking and insurance sales. North Texas has a swift, urban lifestyle.

The state capital, Austin, lies in the heart of Central Texas, a region of rolling hills and hardy farmers. Its most famous citizen was President Lyndon Johnson, who grew up on a dusty ranch at

San Antonio (above), settled long before the Anglos came, retains the flavor of old Mexico. The eighteenth-century Spanish colonial Mission San Francisco de la Espada (right) is an active parish even today.

Johnson City, a town founded by his grandfather. Germans and Czechs settled here generations ago, and their descendants still work the land.

South Texas includes San Antonio and embraces the border area. Mexicans and mestizos settled this region long before the Anglos came, and the flavor of old Mexico remains. Some communities in South Texas are more than 90 percent Mexican American. The presence of Mexican and American cultures lends a unique flavor to South Texas.

West Texas, a land of vast ranches and rich oil fields, had a raw and often violent past. A century ago, if someone was called the "fastest gun west of the Pecos," he was the fastest gun alive. In the west, amateur and professional historians love to talk at length about the colorful frontier days.

Modern Texans move far more frequently than their ancestors did, and the mobility tends to dissolve the regional cultures. Nevertheless, the old question, "Where do you hail from?" carries great impact when asked in Texas.

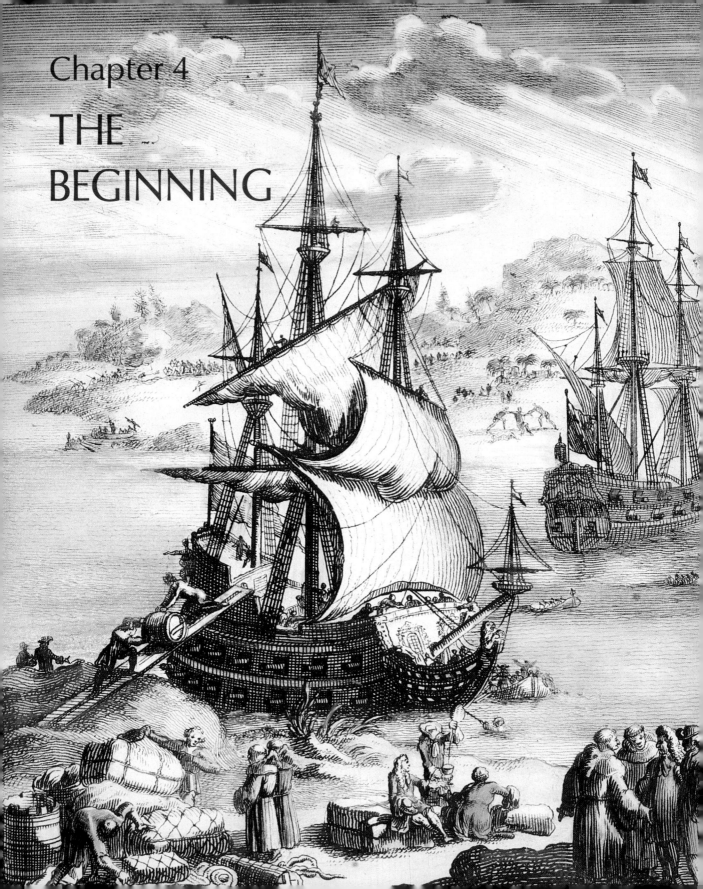

# Chapter 4
# THE
# BEGINNING

# THE BEGINNING

*I live, but I shall not live forever . . .*
*Wonderful Earth, only you live forever.*
—A song sung by the Kiowa people of old Texas

## THE FIRST TEXANS

Between ten thousand and thirteen thousand years ago, nomadic hunters drifted onto the land now called Texas. Those first Texans were descended from the waves of Asian peoples who migrated to North America by crossing a land bridge over the Bering Strait. These prehistoric peoples existed primarily by hunting game and gathering nuts and fruits. In prehistoric times, Texas lands were lush grasslands that could support great numbers of bison.

Modern archaeologists often discover tokens left behind by the prehistoric Texans. Today, there are more than thirty thousand registered archaeological sites in Texas where ancient burial grounds or rock dwellings have been uncovered.

After those early people learned how to grow corn, great civilizations rose on all sides of Texas. In the south, rich societies flourished in Mexico and South America. To the north, the Mound Builders constructed gigantic earthen pyramids and huge human and animal figures. To the west, the Anasazi of present-day New Mexico built remarkable cities. The Indian groups in Texas had mixed progress. Some lived in complex societies, while others remained primitive wanderers.

Panther Cave, whose walls are covered with Indian pictographs,
is one of many archaeological sites on the shores of Lake Amistad.

By the early 1500s, the most advanced of the original Texans
were the tribes of the Caddo Confederacy. The Caddo people lived
comfortably in the Piney Woods of East Texas. Enjoying abundant
rain and rich soil, they grew corn and a wide variety of vegetables,
and they built large, airy houses made of grass, thatch, or
branches. The Caddos were generally a peaceful people.

South and west of the Caddo Confederacy lived a less-advanced
people. Along the Gulf Coast roamed the Karankawas, the
Arkokisas, and the Attacapas. They ate fish and small game, and
perhaps their tastes ranged to other meats. Rival tribes accused the
Karankawas of being cannibals. Farther west in South Texas lived
the Coahuiltecans. Their territory included the Trans-Pecos
Region, where game animals were scarce. Consequently, the
Coahuiltecans learned to eat whatever their dry land offered—
even lizards and rattlesnakes. To the north were the Tonkawas,
whose ancestors had lived in the Great Plains grasslands for
thousands of years. As was true with most Plains Indians, the

In 1528, Spanish explorer Álvar Núñez Cabeza de Vaca was shipwrecked off the Texas coast. During the next eight years, Cabeza de Vaca and three other survivors explored the Southwest.

buffalo was the Tonkawas' staple food. Farther north, the Apaches were relative newcomers in Texas. They were an aggressive, nomadic tribe who looked upon all other tribes as enemies.

## THE EXPLORERS

Spanish sea captain Alonso Álvarez de Piñeda was probably the first European to see Texas shores. In 1519, Piñeda sailed into the mouth of what may have been the Rio Grande, and probably left the ship to make a small excursion into Texas. In 1528, a Spanish ship was lost off the Texas coast. At least four sailors survived— three were Europeans, and the other was a black man named Estevanico. Eight years after they were shipwrecked, the four— having walked more than 2,000 miles (3,219 kilometers)—reached a Spanish fort in northern Mexico. The leader of the party, Álvar Núñez Cabeza de Vaca, claimed that somewhere in the American Southwest stood gleaming cities that were so rich even their poorest inhabitants ate from plates of solid gold. Cabeza de Vaca and his companions had not seen such cities; they were relying on the truth of Indian legends they had heard.

The mention of gold excited dreams in the minds of Spaniards stationed in Mexico, for they had come to the New World hoping to win souls for Christ, to find riches, and to fight with honor on the battlefield. The Spaniards' mission was contained in three words: God, gold, and glory.

Seeking the fabled cities of gold, Francisco de Coronado left Mexico with an army and marched to the American Southwest. Coronado passed through Texas in 1541. As he marched, Coronado met many Indian groups. He demanded that each group swear allegiance to the king of Spain and become Christian. Those who resisted were ruthlessly vanquished in battle. Spanish soldiers carried powerful weapons such as iron swords and thundering muskets. But most important, they fought while riding on horses. To the Indians, horses were incredible animals that seemed to have emerged from another world. It was the horse that allowed Spanish soldiers to dominate the Indians for years to come.

Coronado's expedition found no gold, and Spain quickly lost interest in Texas. Nearly forty years passed before the Spaniards built a small mission church near the site of present-day El Paso. Spain claimed the vast area of Texas, but ruled in name only. There were no other Spanish forts, missions, or settlements in Texas to support Spain's claim to the land.

In 1685, French adventurer René-Robert Cavelier, Sieur de La Salle, established a colony in southeastern Texas. La Salle had done extensive exploring east and west of the Mississippi River. One disaster after another struck the French settlers, and the colony was abandoned after only two years. However, the

Spanish missionaries such as Franciscan Father Antonio Margil de Jesus (left) tried to convert Texas Indians and founded several missions in San Antonio, including Mission Concepción (above).

possibility of a European rival pushing into Spain's territory alarmed the Spaniards. A Spanish effort to colonize Texas began, and a new age dawned on Texas.

## SPANISH MISSIONS AND SETTLEMENT

In 1690, Spaniards built a church and a crude fort along the Neches River in East Texas. The settlement's nearest neighbors were a Caddo tribe called the Hasinai. The people's word for "friend" or "ally" was *Tashas*. The Spaniards had difficulty pronouncing this Indian name, so the priests called their neighbors *Tejas* or *Texas*. Hence the region, and later the state, gained its name.

A second mission was established a short distance away, but it was washed away in a flood a few months later. The original mission fared little better. The mission was far from established

The Alamo was one of the earliest buildings to rise in San Antonio de Bexar.

Spanish outposts and it was difficult to supply. Further, the Indians, susceptible to European diseases, blamed their illnesses on the practices of the missionaries. Without the immediate threat of a nearby French presence, the Spanish lost interest and closed the mission in 1693.

Throughout the 1700s, Spanish interest in establishing permanent settlements in the Texas region continued to wax and wane. One of the more successful colonies was San Antonio de Bexar, founded in 1718. Situated along the cool waters of the San Antonio River, it was, according to a Spanish friar, the "best site in the world, with good and abundant irrigation water, rich lands for pasture, plentiful building stone, and excellent timber." One of the earliest buildings to rise in the settlement—which was to become modern San Antonio—was a thick-walled stone church that was later called the Alamo.

By 1730, the Spaniards had carved a dozen settlements out of the Texas wilderness. Following patterns set elsewhere in the New

World, they attempted to rule Texas Indians with the sword and the cross. At the heart of each settlement was a military fort and a church. Soldiers stationed at the fort protected the Spanish colonists and local, friendly Indians from attacks by the more-aggressive Indian tribes. Meanwhile, the priests worked to convince the Indians to forsake Indian religious beliefs and convert to Catholicism. The Indians taught the Spaniards the best ways to till Texas soil and grow healthy crops. The Indians also taught the colonists how to stalk local game animals and how to preserve their catch.

By 1800, after more than a hundred years of colonization, only about three thousand Spanish colonists and one thousand soldiers lived in Texas. Most of the settlers had migrated north from Mexico, and many were mestizos. More would have ventured into Texas, but the difficult conditions and the fear of Indian attacks discouraged migration.

## LIVESTOCK LEGACY

The Spanish settlement efforts were to result in widespread economic as well as political influence on the Texas region. In 1689, while searching for La Salle's settlement, Captain Alonso de Leon traveled through parts of Central and East Texas. It was his practice to leave a cow and a calf at each river crossing. Also, when the Spanish abandoned their East Texas missions, the mission cattle roamed free. The lean, rangy, longhorned cattle, bred in Mexico, thrived on the Texas grasslands. By the early 1700s, significant numbers of wild cattle were roaming the region.

The Spanish land policies favored large ranches, and cattle ranching soon became an industry in Texas. The cattle ranches helped Spanish Texas to develop a two-tiered society: the

The Spanish ranchers who settled in Texas tried to establish the same extravagant lifestyles enjoyed by the *hacendados* of Mexico. The wealthy hacienda owner in southeastern Mexico shown here with his daughter was riding out to consult with his estate manager.

*hacendado* (owner of the ranch), who lived a relatively luxurious life, and the *vaquero* (cowboy), who worked long hours and ate a meager diet. Most vaqueros endured with few complaints, as this letter from a San Antonio ranch worker attests: "We were of the poor people . . . almost as poor as the Savior in His manger. But we were not dissatisfied. There was time to eat and sleep and watch the plants grow. Of food we did not have overmuch—beans and chili, chili and beans."

It was the Spanish who brought sheep to Texas lands, too. Although not as extensive as cattle ranching, sheep ranching has had an economic impact on Texas.

The romantic image of a herd of wild mustang horses also has Spanish roots. Horses, once plentiful in North America, had become extinct by the time the Spanish explorers and conquistadors arrived. But the Spanish had brought their own fine horses.

With remarkable speed, the Plains Indians became superior horsemen. The horse—the same weapon that once had made the

Artist George Catlin's painting of a Comanche war party dramatizes the widely held belief that the Comanches were the greatest horsemen in the Southwest.

Spaniards invincible—was now turned against the conquerors. The Apaches, cunning warriors on foot, were even more fearsome when mounted on horseback. But the greatest horsemen in the Southwest were the Comanches, a tribe that moved into Texas after the arrival of the Spaniards. Thundering over the grasslands, Comanche warriors became one of history's most famed light cavalry groups. The Comanches moved into lands that had been the domain of the Apaches. Conflicts arose between the two tribes. At the same time, the Apaches moved southward in Texas, displacing the Coahuiltecan. The horse was at the center of the movement of great numbers of people throughout Texas.

Beset by Indian problems and the ever-threatening French presence in neighboring Louisiana, Spanish leaders in Texas gave little notice to another potential enemy far to the east. Beyond Louisiana lay the United States, a young, ambitious, and ever-expanding country hungry for land. Many Americans looked on the vast lands of the Southwest and saw more than just a new frontier. They saw the beginnings of an empire.

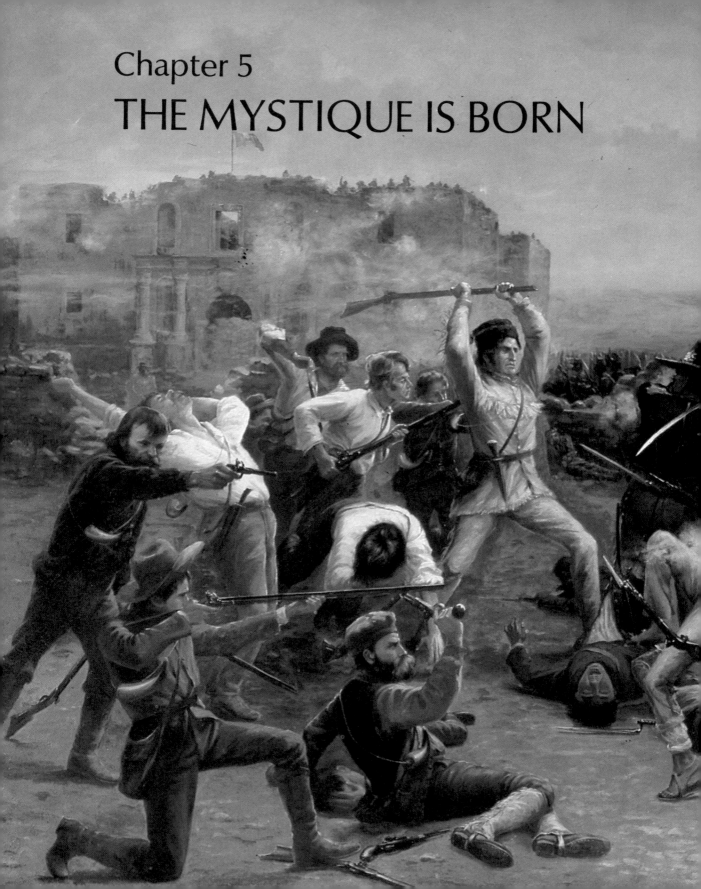

Chapter 5
# THE MYSTIQUE IS BORN

# THE MYSTIQUE IS BORN

*The enemy has demanded a surrender. . . .*
*I have answered their demand with a cannon shot,*
*and our flag still waves proudly from the walls.*
—William Travis, commander of the besieged fortress Alamo

## MEXICO AND THE ANGLOS

In 1820, Missouri businessman Moses Austin crossed Texas, gazing at the fertile but untilled soil. As Austin traveled, plans for starting an Anglo-American farming community took shape in his mind. He discussed his dream with Spanish officials in San Antonio. The officials were wary. They suspected that the Americans were a land-hungry lot, always looking to expand the country's borders. Yet, if a group of American farmers agreed to become Spanish citizens, they could help fight the Indians, tame the raw lands, and strengthen Spanish land claims. With the help of a friend trusted by the Spanish leaders, Austin was granted the land he needed to start a colony.

Moses Austin died shortly after his journey, and the task of establishing the farming community was taken up by his son Stephen. No sooner had the people begun arriving than they learned that Spain had been overthrown and a new government of Mexico ruled Texas. To Austin and the colonists, the change in government meant that they now had to shift their loyalties from Spain to Mexico.

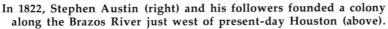

In 1822, Stephen Austin (right) and his followers founded a colony along the Brazos River just west of present-day Houston (above).

In 1822, Austin and his followers began farming along the Brazos River just west of present-day Houston. The colony numbered about three hundred families, known today as the "Old Three Hundred." To be a descendant of those first settlers is a matter of great pride in Texas—in much the way tracing ancestry back to the *Mayflower* is a source of pride in Massachusetts.

A wave of "Texas Fever" struck the American frontier. Pioneers in Tennessee and other southern states left their homes, posted signs reading GTT (Gone to Texas), and journeyed west. Most settlers joined colonies headed by *empresarios* (land agents) who had persuaded the Mexican government to give them enormous tracts of land for settlement. Stephen Austin was Texas's most successful empresario, and he is hailed as the "Father of Texas."

In general, and with much hard work, the Anglo-American colonies did well. All was not perfect, however. The pioneers lived in constant fear of Indian attack. Often the burden of labor fell unequally on the women, who cooked, cleaned, worked the fields, raised children, and worried about the Comanche raids while the men were away on long hunting trips. As one Texan wrote, "Texas was a heaven for men and dogs, but a hell for women and oxen."

Within fifteen years, the Anglos in Texas outnumbered Mexicans four to one. There were about twenty thousand white settlers and four thousand black slaves. Attempts by the Mexican government to stem immigration were fruitless. Texas's reputation continued to draw colonists.

Friction developed between the American community and the Mexican authorities. The Anglos demanded a greater voice in Texas government and they wanted the right to ship and receive goods from gulf ports. Austin had been scrupulous about obeying Mexican law, but the newer empresarios and their settlers often disregarded those laws. For instance, Mexico forbade slavery, and only special loopholes in the law permitted slavery in Texas. Mexican officials began to see the settlers' disregard for laws as the beginning of an open revolt.

## THE TEXAS WAR OF INDEPENDENCE

In 1832, army general Antonio Lopez de Santa Anna seized power in Mexico. He ran the country with an iron fist, and was determined to bring the upstart Texas colonists into line. In 1833, Stephen Austin tried to soothe the differences between the Anglos and the government, but Mexican authorities accused him of treason and threw him in jail. When he was released, the usually patient Austin was resigned to war. "War is our only recourse," he wrote. "No halfway measures, but war in full."

Fighting broke out in the town of Gonzales in 1835, and soon all of Texas was aflame. The conflict involved more than Anglos against Mexicans. Many Mexicans whose families had lived in Texas for generations joined in the fight against the tyrannical Santa Anna. Jose Antonio Navarro, who helped write the Texas Declaration of Independence, was one of the movement's most important figures. Free blacks also rallied to the Texas cause. Indeed, the first blood shed in the war was that of Samuel McCullough, Jr., a black volunteer who was wounded in an early battle.

In February 1836, a Mexican army commanded by Santa Anna marched into San Antonio and surrounded the old walled mission called the Alamo.

Inside the walled fort were 189 defenders. They came from a score of different states and many foreign countries. A dozen were Texas-born Hispanics. Three were known folk heroes: Jim Bowie,

After a fierce attack that lasted thirteen days, Mexican troops led by
Antonio Lopez de Santa Anna (left) killed every one of the defenders of
the Alamo, including Davy Crockett (middle) and James Bowie (right).

the hard-fighting Louisianian; Davy Crockett, the famous
frontiersman; and William Travis, the brave but stubborn outpost
commander. According to legend, Travis called the Alamo
defenders into formation, drew a line in the dirt with his sword,
and announced that all who wished to fight should take one step
forward. All but one of the 189 took the fateful step.

On March 6, 1836, a battle of desperate fury raged in San
Antonio. Outnumbered almost twenty to one, the Texans had no
chance of victory. Yet, three times the men of the Alamo drove the
Mexican army from the walls. According to one Mexican officer,
the Texas artillery "resembled a constant thunder."

Santa Anna ordered his soldiers to take no prisoners. All of the
Alamo defenders were slain. Raw courage and the refusal to give
up a task despite impossible odds is a vital part of the Texas
mystique. The defenders of the Alamo remain as glowing
examples of that mystique.

Only days after the Battle of the Alamo, a Mexican army unit
slaughtered an even larger force of Texans at the town of Goliad.
The two defeats left Texas's forces in shambles.

In the final battle of the Texas revolution, Sam Houston (right) defeated Santa Anna at the Battle of San Jacinto. The general (standing at left, in brown hat and moustache) was captured, and the Texans had won their independence.

Unknown to the defenders of the Alamo, history had been written on March 2, 1836. In the tiny town of Washington-on-the-Brazos, Sam Houston and others signed the Texas Declaration of Independence. The document proclaimed that Texas was an independent nation. But the region, and indeed the lives of all Texans, remained in the hands of Santa Anna.

Sam Houston had distinguished himself in the War of 1812 against the British. In Texas, he had another opportunity to play an important role in history. Houston took command of a ragtag group called the Army of Texas and began to play a masterful cat-and-mouse game with the Mexicans. He retreated, but as he did, Houston's scouts reported the Mexican army's every move. One scout, a tough backwoodsman named Deaf Smith, told Houston that the Mexican soldiers always stopped for a *siesta* (nap) promptly at three o'clock in the afternoon. Houston, noting this practice, continued to withdraw.

On April 21, 1836, on the banks of the San Jacinto River, Houston gathered his men to attack. The Texans crept up to the Mexican camp during the soldiers' siesta. When Houston gave the order to charge, the Texans thundered into the drowsy Mexican camp shouting, "Remember the Alamo!" The Mexicans, caught by surprise, were overwhelmed. Even Santa Anna was taken prisoner, and his surviving soldiers trudged back to Mexico, leaderless and demoralized. The infant Republic of Texas had won a remarkable victory.

## THE LONE STAR EXPERIENCE

Sam Houston served as the republic's first president and Stephen Austin was the first secretary of state. The Republic of Texas was often called the Lone Star Republic, named for the single star that appeared on its flag and on its currency.

The new republic had a variety of challenges and opportunities before it. Settlements faced attack by Indians living within the republic's borders. The threat of re-invasion by the Mexican army was ever-present. Many settlements had been destroyed by war. Shipping manufactured goods into Texas and produce out of the region was difficult, as there were few adequate roads. In addition, the republic's treasury was empty.

Yet, during its ten-year history, the population of the Republic of Texas grew from 35,000 in 1836 to 140,000 in 1847 — an amazing fourfold increase. Land was the country's biggest attraction. The government gave away huge tracts of land to people willing to settle there. The government also passed a revolutionary homestead-exemption law which stated that a citizen's land could not be taken away if he failed to pay his debts.

The majority of the newcomers who flocked to Texas were Americans, but many immigrants came from Europe. Thousands of Germans, fleeing revolutions at home, settled in Central Texas and founded communities such as Fredericksburg and New Braunfels. Settlers came from Belgium, France, England, Ireland, and Sweden. The immigrants came for a variety of reasons. A

The Petri family, who started a farm near New Braunfels, were among the thousands of Germans who settled in Central Texas.

Czech doctor named Maresh said, "They came in order to live their lives as they wished, free from oppression: political, religious, and class."

Lone Star settlers relied primarily on cattle ranching and cotton crops. A prosperous rancher might own as much as 40,000 acres (16,188 hectares) and have a herd numbering twenty thousand head. Cotton planters in East Texas discovered that river bottom land could yield healthy harvests of cotton.

Texas settlers continued to move west into lands claimed by the Apaches, Comanches, and the newly arrived Kiowas. To protect the settlement of Fredericksburg from Comanche raids, the Germans, under the leadership of John Meusebach, negotiated a treaty with the Comanches. The treaty was kept by both sides— the only successful treaty in Texas history.

The Indians in East Texas, such as the Cherokees, bargained in good faith with the settlers. However, Mirabeau B. Lamar, who succeeded Houston as president, recognized no peaceful Indians. He launched a brutal campaign to drive the Cherokees out of the

The celebrated Texas Rangers guarded settlers against Indians, discouraged raids by the Mexican army, and pursued cattle rustlers.

country. In later years, continued hostilities virtually eliminated all the Indians from Texas.

Countless books and movies have celebrated the exploits of the Texas Rangers. Their reputation was well deserved. The first rangers were commissioned by Stephen Austin to guard his settlement against Indian raids. Eventually, Texas Rangers also discouraged raids from the Mexican army and pursued cattle rustlers. On the frontier, it was said that the Texas Rangers "could ride like Mexicans, shoot like Tennesseans, and fight like the very devil."

No more than 5 percent of the people lived in cities during the Lone Star era, but urban areas were beginning to develop. Cities emerged in East and Central Texas, though West Texas remained an undeveloped land for years to come. San Antonio, the old Spanish capital, was the largest town in Texas. Galveston, founded in 1836, was the principal port for receiving European immigrants and shipping out cotton. The town of Houston served for a brief period as the capital. In 1839, construction began at Austin, the new capital city. And in 1841, John Neely Bryan built a home and a store on the Trinity River and called the settlement Dallas.

The Lone Star Republic produced many powerful individuals. Sam Maverick was a rancher and the mayor of San Antonio. He rarely penned his herd, and when his neighbors saw stray cattle, they said, "Those must be Maverick's." To this day, a fiercely independent politician is called a maverick. Another memorable Lone Star figure was Francis Lubbock, a Houston storekeeper who was to serve as governor when Texas became a state. Jose Antonio Navarro, the Texas-born Hispanic, remained a political and intellectual leader of the struggling nation.

## TEXAS BECOMES AMERICAN

When Texas gained its independence from Mexico, Sam Houston hoped the region would become a state. However, statehood was not easy to attain. The Mexican government continued to consider Texas a colony—although rebellious—and threatened war if the United States attempted annexation. Northerners contested the annexation of Texas because they did not want a pro-southern slave state admitted to the American Union. Southerners, aware that slavery had been outlawed in Texas, did not support Texas statehood, either. While Congress debated, Sam Houston set some political machinery in motion. He hinted that if the United States refused to annex Texas, then perhaps Britain or France might do so. Actually, Houston and other Lone Star leaders had little intention of joining a European power, but just the threat shocked Congress into action. On March 1, 1845, Congress voted to annex Texas, and four months later a Texas convention approved the annexation. Texas officially became a state on December 29, 1845.

The annexation agreement included four very important special conditions: (1) Texas was annexed not as a territory, but as a state.

This marked the only time in United States history that a sovereign nation became an American state. (2) All of Texas's public lands were to be retained by the state—not turned over to the federal government. (At the time of annexation, about half of Texas was unclaimed public land.) (3) Texas, if it wished, could divide itself into five different states. No other state enjoyed that privilege. (4) Texas had to pay all the debts it accumulated as an independent republic.

Mexico was true to its threats, and annexation resulted in a war between the United States and Mexico. The war raged between 1846 and 1848, with most of the battles fought on Mexican soil. The peace treaty forced Mexico to give up all her claims on the American Southwest as well as California.

Soon after the war, a border dispute between Texas and the federal government developed. Texas claimed much of the Southwest as its own. As part of a Congressional act called the Compromise of 1850, Texas dropped its claims on New Mexico in exchange for $10 million. Texas used the money to pay the many debts left over from its Lone Star experience. The state's northern and western borders were fixed as they now stand.

## THE CIVIL WAR

The joy and pride of Texas's statehood were soon clouded by the wrenching issues of secession and slavery. Most Texans allied themselves with the southern viewpoint—many had come to Texas from the South. One notable exception was Sam Houston. Houston traveled the state speaking out against secession from the American Union; he believed that seceding from the United States could lead to war.

In February 1861, despite Houston's stirring speeches, the

Though European immigrants to Texas despised slavery, those settlers who came from the Deep South brought slaves with them to work on their farms.

people of Texas voted to secede and join the Confederacy. Houston, who had been elected governor a year earlier, refused to take an oath of allegiance to the Confederacy, preferring instead to vacate the office of governor.

More than seventy thousand Texans served the Confederate cause. Texas was the site of the last Civil War battle: on May 11, 1865, nearly a month after Confederate General Robert E. Lee's surrender to Union General Ulysses S. Grant, Confederate troops were victorious in an engagement at Palmito Ranch near Brownsville.

The years immediately following the Civil War were harsh in Texas. Although Texas lands did not suffer the degree of devastation witnessed throughout the South, the state was in turmoil. Federal troops occupied Texas during the Reconstruction period, yet lawlessness was widespread. Outlaw elements were active throughout the state. Indian attacks were common along the state's western frontier. And racial violence, fed by the radical reforms and organizations such as the Ku Klux Klan, was rampant. Texas would have to draw on the strength of its people in order to survive the chaos.

# Chapter 6
# FROM CATTLE KINGS TO OIL BARONS

# FROM CATTLE KINGS TO OIL BARONS

*Oh say, little dogie, when will you lay down,*
*And give up this shifting and roving around?*
*My horse is leg weary, and I'm awfully tired,*
*But if you get away, I'm sure to be fired.*
*Lay down, little dogie, lay down.*
—A cowhand range song

## THE COWBOY ERA

After the Civil War, Texas's state treasury was empty, again.
The state's prewar economy had depended on slaves and land.
The former slaves were now free, and land prices had begun to
drop. Cotton—always vital to the state's economy—was a
demanding crop, requiring much work and many laborers.
However, Texas did have an untapped resource—cattle. An
estimated four million head of longhorns roamed the ranges in
the south. In Texas, the cattle were worth about four dollars a
head; they were sources of tallow and hide. Meanwhile, northern
cities were willing to pay as much as forty dollars a head for the
cattle, which would provide a source of food. The task was clear:
drive the cattle north. Small-scale cattle drives to northern
markets had taken place for years, but in 1866, the great trail
drives began. In that year alone, more than a quarter of a million
cattle were driven to market. Those drives launched the legendary
era of the cowboy.

To push a herd from Texas to railroad depots in Kansas or Missouri meant a trek of 1,000, or even 1,500, miles (1,609 to 2,414 kilometers). Such a journey took a "trail outfit" three to six months to complete. The drives usually traveled on routes such as the Chisholm Trail, which had been established by a Cherokee trader. Herd after herd crossed the fenceless plains.

Cattle drives involved painful, hard work, and often danger. A cowboy worked long days; five hours of sleep was a luxury. River crossings were particularly difficult, and stampedes struck terror in everyone's heart. Contrary to western movies, cowboys taking the northern route rarely faced warring Indians. The Indians who did approach cattle drives usually came to trade goods or to demand "grass rental" for allowing the cattle to pass through their territory. There were times when the trail outfits had to fight off cattle rustlers—some white, some Indian.

Cowboys came from many walks of life; at least one in three post-Civil War Texas cowboys was either Mexican or black. The cowhands were superb horsemen; their favorite mount was the quarter horse. It was said that a good quarter horse could "turn on a dime and give you change."

Ranch owners, too, needed extraordinary courage and strength. Richard King, a transplanted New Yorker, owned the King Ranch, a ranch as large as the entire state of Rhode Island. Lizzie Johnson owned vast ranch lands near Austin. She often traveled on trail drives, and gained the cowhands' respect with what they called "Miss Lizzie's" toughness. Perhaps the most daring of the ranch owners was Charles Goodnight, who established ranches in the dry-as-dust Panhandle region where the Apaches and Comanches were active. Goodnight, with his partner Oliver Loving, blazed a new cattle trail that ran west of the Pecos River, through New Mexico, and into Colorado.

Though the romance of the cowboy era was legendary, the daily life of a cowboy had few frills. Branding cattle (above) and taking meals from an outdoor chuck wagon (right) were part of a cowhand's routine. Below: Black cowboys at a fair in Bonham

The great cattle-drive period lasted only about twenty years. Perhaps as many as forty thousand Americans served as cowpunchers on the drives. By the 1880s, barbed-wire fences crisscrossed open ranges, and railroads snaked across Texas, making the drives both impossible and unnecessary. But those two decades of trail drives captured the imagination of the world and provided more than a century of legend.

By 1875, most Great Plains Indians, including Apaches such as these, were forced to move to reservations in present-day Oklahoma.

## SETTLEMENT OF THE WEST

In the post-Civil War years, Texas once again enjoyed rapid population growth. The population was concentrated in the eastern half of the state, but during the early 1870s, a great push to settle West Texas and the Panhandle began. Battles with Indians broke out at sites such as Salt Creek, Howard Wells, and Adobe Walls. To subdue the Indians, the state militia as well as federal troops and Texas Rangers arrived in the Great Plains.

By 1875, most Great Plains Indians, such as the Apaches, Comanches, and Kiowas, were forced to move to reservations in present-day Oklahoma. The cavalry constantly pursued the Indians and white hunters wantonly slaughtered buffaloes, the Indians' staple food. By the mid-1880s, only a few small bands of Texas's original inhabitants remained.

Freed from Indian fears, pioneer ranchers and farmers poured into Great Plains lands. Within thirty years, the Texas Great Plains

Windmills were used on the Great Plains of Texas to pump water for cattle, for farm irrigation, and for the locomotives that crisscrossed the state in the late 1800s.

population grew from only a handful to half a million. Although rainfall in the west was sparse, farmers discovered that the Texas Great Plains had vast reserves of underground water. Also, an almost constant breeze swept across the western flatlands. Together, the water and wind made windmills an obvious choice for power and water. The whirling giants became as common on West Texas plains as television antennas are today.

Railroads, more than any other enterprise, were vital to the settling of West Texas and the Panhandle. By 1890, nearly 9,000 miles (14,484 kilometers) of track sprawled across the state. The three well-traveled lines that ran through the western part of the state linked the frontier to East Texas, to neighboring states, to the East Coast, and to the West Coast. Another line began at Fort Worth and snaked over the Panhandle to serve such developing towns as Childress, Clarendon, Amarillo, and Dalhart.

The railroads were a mixed blessing for the struggling Texas farmers and ranchers. Railroad owners often made secret

Chapter 7

# TOWARD NEW FRONTIERS

Antonio, F
oil wells p
needs. The
churned o

About 7
forces dur
war's mos


Perhaps
War II tha
state into
of the pec
shipbuild
industry
technolog

Texas i
1958, Jacl
discovery
resulted i
this adva
compute:

In the
the state
apparent
low tide,
land belc
importai
oil. In 19
tideland

# TOWARD NEW FRONTIERS

*Houston . . . the eagle has landed.*
—Astronaut Neil Armstrong, upon landing
on the surface of the moon

## DEPRESSION AND WAR

While oil brought giddy wealth to a few Texans, most small farmers, ranchers, and industrial workers struggled to make ends meet during the early twentieth century. The Great Depression of the 1930s increased the plight of the poorer people of Texas. In 1932, more than three hundred thousand workers in the state were unemployed. Farmers were ruined by plummeting crop prices. Cotton, which sold for eighteen cents a pound in 1928, dropped to six cents in 1931. A stubborn drought, combined with years of overgrazing, turned much of the Panhandle into a sea of dust, driving farmers and ranchers from their Great Plains homes.

During the depression, Texans' attention focused on the always lively world of Texas politics. The state's tradition of self-reliance was being tested. Miriam A. "Ma" Ferguson, the wife of former governor James Ferguson, had been governor from 1925 to 1927, and was elected to a second term in 1933. During her second term, Governor Ferguson worked to establish relief programs for the unemployed and destitute, and conservation programs for the state's farmlands. The programs added to the state's financial problems—at one point Governor Ferguson assumed

**Governor**

respons
term as
Ku Klu
enacted
retirem

In W
formul
countr
served
Roosev
chaired
Buchar
same t
distrib

Dur
More
Lone S

Chapter 8

# GOVERNMENT AND THE ECONOMY

# GOVERNMENT AND THE ECONOMY

*I don't know what the word failure means.*
*Temporary setback, I'll buy. I've had those.*
*But I don't fail.*
—Texas businessman Jimmy Dean

## THE GOVERNMENT

Texas is governed by provisions written in its 1876 constitution. To change, or amend, the constitution requires a two-thirds vote of the state legislature and the approval of a majority of the state's voters. The state government is divided into three branches: the legislative, which is responsible for creating laws; the executive, which is responsible for carrying out laws; and the judicial, which tries cases and is responsible for interpreting laws.

The executive branch is headed by the governor, who is elected to a four-year term. The constitution empowers the governor to act as commander-in-chief of the military forces of the state, meaning that he or she may call out the state militia in times of emergency. The governor of Texas is allowed to appoint two important executive officers—the secretary of state and the adjutant general. The governors of most states have far greater powers of appointment. Other Texas executive officers, such as the lieutenant governor, the commissioner of agriculture, and the comptroller, are elected by the people.

The legislative branch consists of two houses: a 31-member

senate and a 150-member house of representatives. Senators are elected to four-year terms; the members of the house serve two years. Legislators discuss proposed laws, called bills. When they approve a bill, it is sent to the governor for his or her signature. The governor may refuse to sign a bill, in which case the bill is returned to the legislators. Then, if both legislative houses approve the bill by a two-thirds margin, the bill becomes a law regardless of the governor's wishes.

The judicial branch consists of the state court system. The highest court is the supreme court, which has a chief justice and eight associate members, all of whom are elected to six-year terms. The nine-member court of criminal appeals is the state's second-strongest judicial body. Other courts hear a broad range of criminal and civil cases.

The state's 254 counties and nearly 1,200 incorporated cities and villages make up its local government complex. Local governments have vital responsibilities such as maintaining schools, building local roads, and funding parks, playgrounds, and police departments.

## EDUCATION

Texans have a tradition of strongly supporting their school system. Nearly 3.5 million elementary and secondary students attend Texas schools. The average public school has about seventeen students for each teacher. More than 40 percent of the state's total budget is used for education. Much of the money for the state's school system comes from a school fund established in 1876 and from oil industry taxes.

A dropout problem plagues the school system, but officials try to keep standards high. In 1985, Texas was first to pass a statewide

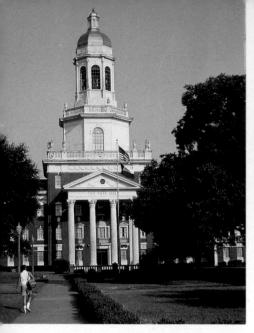

Baylor University at Waco (left), is privately funded.
The University of Texas, with campuses at Austin (above)
as well as six other cities, is funded by the state.

"no pass, no play" law forbidding a student with failing grades to participate in extracurricular activities.

Texas is home to many outstanding private and public universities and colleges. The state-funded University of Texas system is a network of seven schools with campuses at Austin, Arlington, Dallas, El Paso, Odessa, San Antonio, and Tyler. The sprawling Austin campus is the largest of these schools, with an enrollment of about fifty thousand. Other large state university systems are Texas A & M and the University of Houston. Important privately funded colleges include Abilene Christian at Abilene, Baylor at Waco, Rice at Houston, Southern Methodist University at Dallas, Texas Christian University at Fort Worth, and Texas Tech at Lubbock.

## MANUFACTURING

About 15 percent of Texas workers are engaged in manufacturing; they produce goods that account for 16 percent of the state's gross product. For years, Texas has ranked among the top ten states in factory production. Texas plants produce pumps

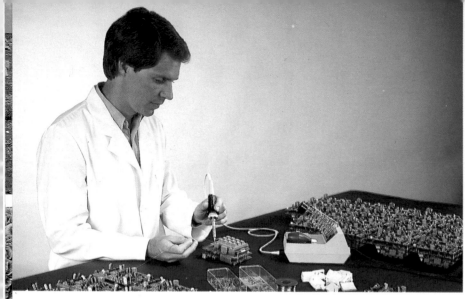

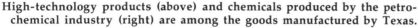

High-technology products (above) and chemicals produced by the petro-chemical industry (right) are among the goods manufactured by Texas.

and drilling equipment for use in the oil fields. Construction equipment and refrigeration and heating machinery are among the state's other products. Chief manufacturing centers include Dallas-Fort Worth, Houston, Lubbock, Odessa, and San Antonio.

In processing facilities near the Gulf Coast, crude oil is made into chemicals that in turn become house paints and farm fertilizers. Texas is the nation's largest producer of chemicals.

The state's food-processing industry works closely with its farms. Food-processing plants bottle beverages, package meat, can fruit and vegetables, polish rice, and prepare dozens of other farm-grown products for the stores. In the Panhandle and Southern High Plains regions, large meat-processing plants are located in Friona, Plainview, and Hereford.

Oil-rich Texas leads the states in refining crude oil into a variety of petroleum and petroleum-based products. Refineries are located throughout the state, but the largest are along the Gulf Coast in cities such as Baytown, Beaumont, Houston, and Port Arthur.

High-technology goods are the state's newest industry. These products range from hand-held calculators to ultra-sophisticated spacecraft and guided missiles. Today, the nearly 8,000 high-tech

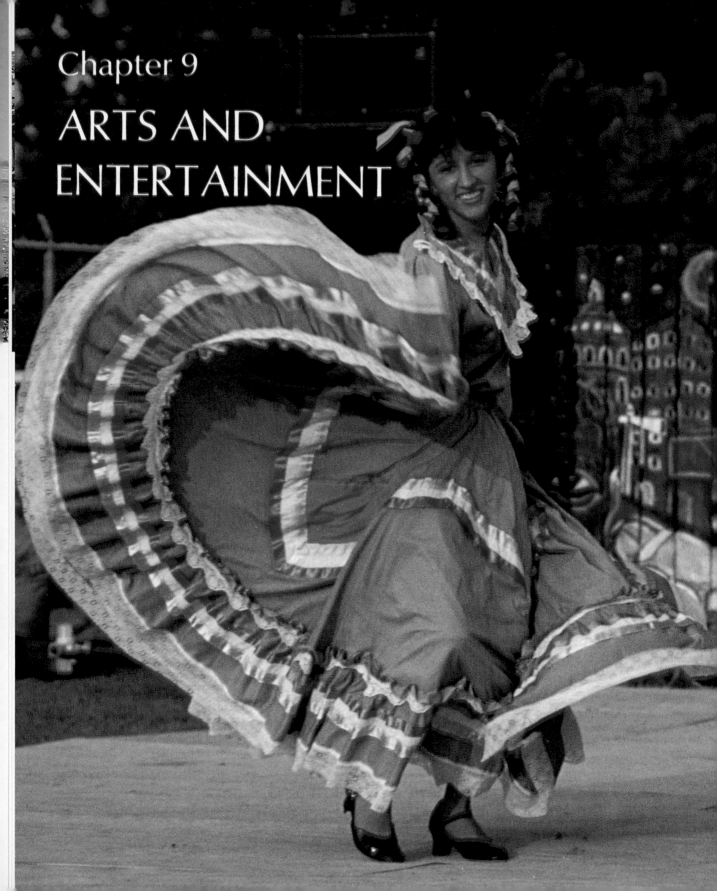

# Chapter 9

# ARTS AND ENTERTAINMENT

Chapter 10

# A TOUR OF TEXAS

# A TOUR OF TEXAS

It would require a lifetime to see all that Texas has to offer.
However, a quick tour might take a region-by-region approach.
One thing to remember while touring the state is that Texas is
squeaky clean. Texans do not tolerate littering. Everywhere in the
state, signs warn: DON'T MESS WITH TEXAS.

## NORTH TEXAS

North Texas, which centers on the Dallas-Fort Worth area, is a
region wrapped up in a "big-city" way of life. But the north has
many quaint and quiet small towns, and it harbors spectacular
natural scenery.

Wichita Falls, near the Oklahoma border, is the gateway to
North Texas. The well-rounded town is an industrial center with
its own symphony orchestra, ballet, and community theater.
Nearby Denton is the home of North Texas State University and
Texas Woman's University, the nation's largest women's college.
Aviation buffs flock to Denton to see vintage World War I and
World War II aircraft at the Fighting Air Command Flying
Museum.

Three dozen major lakes dot North Texas, and many of them
have adjoining state parks and campgrounds. Possum Kingdom
Lake is the region's most popular. Hikers and picnickers enjoy the
surrounding Possum Kingdom State Park. Lavon Lake, near the
city of Rockwall, attracts boaters and swimmers.

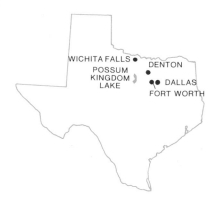

Left: The Bloom Festival at the Dallas Arboretum and Botanical Garden

Approaching Dallas, visitors wonder why they built such a big city way out here in the country. The city simply sprouts out of flat prairie land—for no apparent reason. Dallas was founded by John Neely Bryan as a trading post, and vigorous trade has nurtured its growth. Dallas stores vary from high-volume wholesale outlets to elegant stores such as Neiman-Marcus. Texas writer A.C. Green once said, "Dallas is where you can get things."

Citizens of Dallas pursue culture and entertainment enthusiastically. There are 271 parks in the city. In State Fair Park stand the Museum of Natural History, the Aquarium, the Age of Steam Museum, the Southwest Museum of Science and Technology, and a majestic shrine called the Hall of State, which honors heroes of Texas history. Near the downtown district is the Dallas Arboretum and Botanical Garden, a refuge of flowers and woodlands interwoven with footpaths. The Dallas Museum of African-American Life and Culture houses displays of African culture and artwork.

Arlington, a Dallas suburb, is home to the Six Flags Over Texas theme park, with an array of dizzying rides. The Texas Rangers

Fort Worth sights include the Water Garden (above), a delightful place to stroll, and the Old Court House (right).

play baseball at Arlington, while nearby Irving is home to the Dallas Cowboys.

Fort Worth is an industrial center anchored by aviation plants such as General Dynamics and Bell Helicopter. The downtown Water Garden, a delightful place to stroll, is a complex series of steps and inclines all flowing with water. Fort Worth's museum district is home to four museums: the Amon Carter Museum of Western Art displays works by such masters of the frontier era as Frederic Remington and Charles Russell; the concrete and glass Kimball Art Museum holds artworks by European and Asian artists; the Fort Worth Museum of Science and Industry has, among other treasures, a superb display on Texas history; and brilliant modern paintings hang at the Fort Worth Art Museum.

## EAST TEXAS AND THE GULF COAST

Texarkana, in the northeast corner of the state, is really two cities, one in Texas and the other in Arkansas. Tourists snapping pictures of Texarkana's historic post office can stand on the

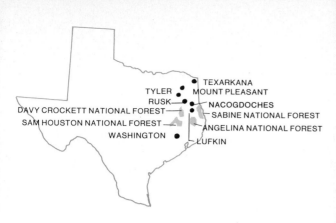

This replica of Independence Hall,
where the Texas Declaration of
Independence was signed, stands in
Washington-on-the-Brazos State Park.

borderline with one foot in each state. The East Texas city of Tyler, which produces half the nation's rose bushes, calls itself the "Rose Capital of the World." Mount Pleasant is a popular vacation town famed for the superb bass fishing at nearby lakes.

East Texas was the location of much of the state's early history, and today the past is always present in the region. Thousands of years ago, Nacogdoches was an Indian village. French explorer La Salle visited it in 1687, a Spanish mission was founded there in 1716, and the town served as a gateway to Texas during Anglo pioneer times. The Texas Declaration of Independence was signed at the East Texas city of Washington (also called Washington-on-the-Brazos, or Old Washington). Texas history is remembered at Washington's Star of the Republic Museum.

East Texas is graced by the Piney Woods, and all four of the state's national forests are in the east. Near the city of Lufkin is the long and narrow Texas State Railroad Park, where tourists hop aboard a century-old train and take a trip through the heart of the Piney Woods. The Jim Hogg State Historical Park, near the town of Rusk, is dedicated to one of the state's most beloved

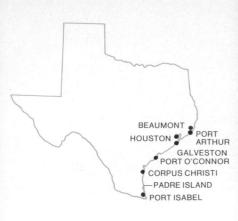

**The Houston skyline at dusk, as seen from Buffalo Bayou Park**

governors. People seeking unspoiled wilderness visit the Sam Houston National Forest and trek over its many miles of deep-woods hiking trails.

The Gulf Coast town of Beaumont experienced Texas's first oil boom, and the boom days can be revisited at the Spindletop Museum and the Lucas Gusher Monument. Nearby Port Arthur is the home of many Acadian, or Cajun, people who immigrated there from Louisiana. Port Arthur is known throughout the West for its outstanding Cajun and seafood restaurants.

Houston, the state's largest city, also boasts the most recent growth. Downtown buildings erected before 1960 are few, and the city skyline looks like a glass-and-steel army. Houston is home to the Lyndon B. Johnson Space Center and the complex of hospitals called the Texas Medical Center. The city's Museum of Fine Arts receives a quarter of a million visitors each year. The Museum of Natural Science features a 232-seat planetarium. Houston's roofed stadium, the Astrodome, is so big that an eighteen-story building could fit inside it. The battleship *Texas*, a veteran of two World Wars, is moored permanently on the waterfront of San Jacinto Battleground State Park.

South Padre Island (left) and Galveston (above), as well as many other Gulf Coast areas, attract vacationers who enjoy swimming, boating, deep-sea fishing, and other water sports.

The island city of Galveston is a busy shipping port, and with miles of accessible beaches, serves as a magnet for tourists. Galveston also has a host of historic homes and churches. However, much of the city had to be rebuilt after the devastating hurricane of 1900.

The Texas Gulf Coast consists of 367 miles (591 kilometers) of beaches dotted by towns and parklands and highlighted by long, narrow islands. Near Port O'Connor is the Matagorda Island State Park, home to a fantastic variety of sea birds. The Aransas National Wildlife Refuge, near Rockport, is the winter meeting grounds for the nearly extinct whooping crane.

With more than a quarter of a million people, beautiful Corpus Christi is the Gulf Coast's largest city. Its Bayfront Arts and Sciences Park holds an art museum, a natural-history museum, and a community theater. The city's Museum of Oriental Cultures displays Asian paintings and sculpture.

The Padre Island National Seashore rings Padre Island. Parks and resorts stand at either end of the island, but the middle is an unblemished nature refuge open to hikers and beachcombers. Tiny Port Isabel is a picturesque village on the southern end of the Gulf Coast.

Austin, in the heart of Central Texas, is the state capital.

## CENTRAL TEXAS

Central Texas is often called the state's backyard. It is a region of small towns, farms, and ranches, and has a special charm.

Guadalupe River State Park, near Boerne, welcomes visitors with scenic hill country washed by the Guadalupe River. In Boerne is the Cave Without a Name, so called because a 1939 naming contest was won by a boy who wrote, "This cave is too pretty to name." Other fascinating Central Texas caves include Inner Space, near Georgetown; Longhorn, near Burnet; Natural Bridge Caverns, near New Braunfels; and Wonder Cave, near San Marcos.

Central Texas, settled more than a century ago by European immigrants, maintains many Old World traditions. Fredericksburg began as a German colony in 1846, and townspeople often dress in peasant costumes and hold saengerfests (songfests). The contributions of Czech settlers are highlighted at the Czech Heritage Museum in Temple. The tiny village of Panna Maria, settled by Poles in 1850, claims to be home to the nation's oldest Polish Roman Catholic Church.

There are many special sights throughout Central Texas. Waco's most popular attraction is the Texas Ranger Hall of Fame, which displays firearms and other relics used by the men who tamed Texas's raw frontier. Johnson City, the birthplace of Lyndon Johnson, offers guided tours of the frame house where the president grew up. The Cowboy Artists of America Museum in Kerrville displays paintings, sculpture, and crafts produced by western American artists.

The city of Austin, in the heart of Central Texas, radiates out from the massive State Capitol building. The white-columned Governor's Mansion stands nearby, and the University of Texas campus is a short walk away. A campus landmark is the Lyndon B. Johnson Library and Museum, which displays a replica of the Oval Office in the White House. Austin's Elisabet Ney Museum features the work of the nineteenth-century artist. Austin streets harbor architectural surprises such as the Greek Revival Neill-Cochran House and the hundred-year-old Driskill Hotel.

## SOUTH TEXAS

"All Texans have two home towns: the one they are living in and San Antonio," is an old saying in the Lone Star State. San Antonio is Texas's heart, soul, and its roots. The Alamo is the city's most visited shrine. A short walk from the Alamo is the Institute of Texan Cultures—a sort of Texas family album—where displays show the accomplishments of Mexican Texans, African-American Texans, German Texans, and other groups. San Antonio's Mexican market, *El Mercado*, is a colorful collection of dozens of small shops and half a dozen restaurants. Mission San

# FACTS AT A GLANCE

## GENERAL INFORMATION

**Statehood:** December 29, 1845; twenty-eighth state

**Origin of Name:** From a Caddo Indian word, *Tejas,* meaning friends or allies

**State Capital:** Austin

**State Nickname:** Lone Star State

**State Flag:** Texas has a red, white, and blue flag. The left one-third of the flag is a blue vertical stripe with a lone white star in the center. The right two-thirds has a single white horizontal stripe atop a single red horizontal stripe. Red represents bravery, white stands for strength, and blue symbolizes loyalty. The flag was adopted in 1839.

**State Motto:** Friendship

**State Bird:** Mockingbird

**State Tree:** Pecan

**State Flower:** Bluebonnet

**State Gem:** Topaz

**State Stone:** Palmwood

**State Grass:** Sideoats grama

**State Shell:** Lightning whelk

**State Dish:** Chili

**Sunset at Lake Texoma, a huge reservoir shared with Oklahoma**

forms the entire southern Texas border from New Mexico to the Gulf of Mexico. The Red River forms the boundary with Oklahoma, and the Sabine forms the eastern border with Louisiana. The Pecos River in West Texas is the major tributary of the Rio Grande. Other major rivers are the Canadian, which flows through the Panhandle; the San Antonio, which flows through San Antonio; the Brazos, which flows through Dallas and Waco; the Nueces, which flows through South Texas; the Colorado, which flows through Central Texas; and the Trinity, which flows through East Texas. All of Texas's rivers either empty directly into the Gulf of Mexico or are tributaries of rivers that empty into the gulf.

**Lakes:** Texas has thousands of lakes, ranging from small ponds to major bodies of water. Many of these lakes have been artificially created to irrigate farmland or provide flood control. Toledo Bend Reservoir, the largest in the state, extends 65 mi. (105 km) along the Louisiana border and has 650 mi. (1,046 km) of shoreline. Lake Texoma, a huge reservoir shared with Oklahoma, has a shoreline of 580 mi. (933 km). Other large artificially created lakes include Amistad, Belton, Buchanan, Eagle Mountain, Falcon, and Sam Rayburn.

**Coast:** Texas has one of the longest seacoasts of the United States. It stretches 367 mi. (591 km) from Louisiana to Mexico. There are thirteen deep-water ports and fifteen ports for barges and ships along the coast.

**The Chihuahuan desert blooms near Van Horn, in the rocky, arid Trans-Pecos Region.**

**Topography:** Texas contains four major land areas: the West Gulf Coastal Plains, the North Central Plains, the Great Plains, and the Trans-Pecos Region.

The West Gulf Coastal Plains is a fertile lowland that covers the southeastern one-third of the state. Much of the land is well-suited to farming, fruit growing, or cattle grazing. This area includes the Piney Woods, a timber range in the eastern portion of the state. The Balcones Escarpment, a geological fault line, forms the western edge of the plain. It separates East Texas from the drier regions of Central and West Texas.

The North Central Plains cover the center of Texas and the eastern half of the Panhandle. The plains are generally treeless. They can be described as a region of hilly belts separated by valley troughs. The plains rise gradually from an elevation of 750 ft. (229 m) to 2,500 ft. (762 m).

West of the North Central Plains lies the Great Plains, an extension of the vast prairie that extends to North Dakota and Canada. These plains rise from 2,700 ft. (823 m) to more than 4,000 ft. (1,219 m) above sea level. This region includes an area along the Mexican border known as the *Llano Estacado,* or High Plains. This is the high, arid land often filmed in cowboy movies. Farmers now irrigate much of the area and grow crops.

The Trans-Pecos Region covers the westernmost part of Texas. Aside from the busy city of El Paso, most of this region is beautiful, but rocky and arid with only sparse vegetation. Guadalupe Peak, the highest point in Texas, is here.

A spreading live oak tree at a cattle ranch near Schulenberg

**Climate:** Western movies usually show Texas as a hot, dry state. But a typical Texas year may find winter blizzards in the northern plains, summer hot spells throughout the state, tornadoes, and perhaps even hurricanes.

The eastern plains generally receive more rainfall than western regions. Houston sees about 45 in. (114 cm), while El Paso, at the western end of the state, gets less than 10 in. (25 cm). Romero received a record 65 in. (165 cm) of snow in the winter of 1923-24. Brownsville, the southernmost city, has not had measurable snow in the twentieth century.

Temperatures vary from north to south. The Panhandle sees winter temperatures that average 35° F. (1.7° C). The state's lowest temperature was recorded in this region: -23° F. (-30.6° C) at Tulia on February 12, 1899 and at Seminole on February 9, 1933. Summer temperatures in the Panhandle average 79° F. (26.1° C).

Southern Texas, especially the Rio Grande Valley, has the warmest weather in the state. Winter temperatures average 60° F. (15.6° C) and summer temperatures average 85° F. (29.4° C). The highest temperature ever recorded was 120° F. (48.9° C) at Seymour on August 12, 1936.

Storms occasionally ravage Texas. A deadly tornado blew through Wichita Falls in 1979, killing 42 people and injuring 1,740 others. A 1987 twister killed 29 people in Saragosa. Hurricanes sometimes wreak havoc on the Gulf Coast. The nation's worst natural disaster was the hurricane that destroyed Galveston in 1900, killing 6,000 people.

## NATURE

**Trees:** Pecan, pine, walnut, hickory, oak, cypress, palm, cedar, gum, juniper, cottonwood, and cat's-claw are among the two hundred kinds of trees found in Texas. Dogwood and magnolia trees beautify many East Texas yards.

Many varieties of cactus, sagebrush, mesquite, and chaparral grow in the dry western regions of the state.

**Wild Plants:** More than five hundred varieties of grasses grow in Texas, mostly in the prairies of the eastern and central regions of the state. These include bluestem, buffalo grass, and sideoats grama. The more than four thousand types of wildflowers in Texas include goldenrods, asters, daisies, and sunflowers. Bluebonnets turn much of Texas into a sea of blue in the springtime. Yucca, century plants, and many varieties of cactus, mesquite, sagebrush, huisache, greasewood, and chaparral grow in drier western regions.

**Animals:** Pronghorn antelopes, armadillos, white-tailed and mule deer, beavers, coyotes, Barbary sheep, opossums, rabbits, foxes, raccoons, bats, and wild pigs are among the many Texas mammals. Reptiles include lizards, alligators, and more than a hundred species of snakes, including four kinds of poisonous snakes.

**Birds:** Nearly 550 species of birds can be found in Texas. Many, such as ducks, geese, and the rare whooping crane, are migratory birds passing along the flyways that cross the state. Wild turkeys, quail, and doves are important game birds. Golden eagles, southern bald eagles, hawks, and owls are major predators. The songful mockingbird is the Texas state bird. Warblers, scissor-tailed flycatchers, prairie chickens, and roadrunners also inhabit the state.

**Fish:** Texas commercial seafood fishermen harvest shrimp as the major seafood "crop," but oysters and crabs also are important. Gulf of Mexico sportsmen catch trout, mackerel, marlin, bonito, red snapper, drum, sailfish, flounder, and grouper. Freshwater fishermen try to land bass, crappie, bluegills, walleye, rainbow trout, and northern pike.

## GOVERNMENT

The government of Texas, like that of the federal government, is divided into three branches: executive, legislative, and judicial. The state legislature, elected by the voters, is responsible for making the laws. It consists of a 150-member house and a 31-member senate. State senators serve four-year terms and state representatives serve two-year terms. The legislature meets in odd-numbered years the second Tuesday in January. Regular sessions are limited by law to 140 days, although special sessions may be called.

The executive branch is headed by the governor, who is elected to a four-year term. The governor appoints the secretary of state and the adjutant general. Voters elect a lieutenant governor, attorney general, commissioner of agriculture, commissioner of the general land office, comptroller, and treasurer. The three members of the Texas Railroad Commission, which also regulates the state's petroleum industry, are also elected.

The judicial branch, which interprets the laws, consists of the court system. The highest court is the supreme court, which has a chief justice and eight associate justices. The highest criminal court is the court of criminal appeals. It has nine justices. Members of these courts are elected to six-year terms.

Texas has fourteen supreme judicial districts. Each of these districts has a court of appeals. Each court of appeals has one chief justice, who serves for a six-year term; the number of associate justices varies.

District courts are the chief trial courts. Each district judge is elected to a four-year term. Other trial courts include county, municipal, justice of the peace, and criminal district courts. Judges of these courts are elected to four-year terms. Most municipal-court judges are elected to two-year terms.

**Number of Counties:** 254

**U.S. Representatives:** 27

**Electoral Votes:** 29

**Voting Qualifications:** Eighteen years of age, state resident for one year, county and district resident for six months

## EDUCATION

Texas maintains one of the largest public school systems in the country, with more than 1,000 public school districts. Nearly 3.5 million students attend Texas elementary and secondary schools. The average public school student-teacher ratio is one teacher for every seventeen students. The state spends about $2,100 per year to educate each student.

The Lone Star State has about sixty-five colleges and universities. The largest university by far is the University of Texas, with campuses in seven cities. Its largest campus, in Austin, enrolls about fifty thousand students; other campuses

**An oil drilling rig in Houston**

are located in Arlington, Dallas, El Paso, Odessa, San Antonio, and Tyler. Other large public universities include Texas A & M at College Station, Texas Tech at Lubbock, Texas Woman's University at Denton, and the University of Houston.

Texas also has many noted private colleges and universities. These include Abilene Christian in Abilene, Baylor in Waco, Rice at Houston, Southern Methodist University at Dallas, Texas Christian University at Fort Worth, and Trinity University at San Antonio.

## ECONOMY AND INDUSTRY

**Principal Products:**

*Agriculture:* Cotton, cattle and calves, sorghum grain, wheat, rice, poultry, hogs, turkeys, hay, vegetables, cottonseed, and citrus fruits

*Manufacturing:* Cotton processing, meat packing, food processing, production of machinery, oil refining, petrochemicals, electronics products, and high-technology goods

*Natural Resources:* Oil, natural gas, sulfur, helium, gypsum, clay, and salt. Forests cover 14 percent of the state.

**Business and Trade:** Texas is rich and diversified. If it were independent, it would be one of the world's wealthiest nations. More than 70 percent of working Texans (more than 4 million people) are employed in service industries. Another 15 percent (nearly 1 million) work in manufacturing industries. Agriculture employs about 200,000 workers (1 percent), and mining employs 266,000.

Every region of Texas specializes in different products. East Texas relies on its natural resources, such as wood, oil, sulfur, and natural gas. Agricultural products also play an important role there. In North Texas, the city of Dallas is one of the leading banking and insurance centers in the South, while Fort Worth is a railroad center so famed for its cattle that Texans call it "Cow Town." The Plains and Panhandle rely on agriculture made possible by irrigation to grow cotton,

117

sorghum, wheat, corn, and other feed grains. The Plains cities of Midland and Odessa are major oil centers. Central Texas has many service industries as well as rich farmland. Military bases employ many persons there. The government and the University of Texas are major employers in Austin. Oil and petrochemical products dominate the Gulf Coast economy. Nearby Houston, the nation's fourth-largest city, has a diversified economy.

**Communication:** Ever since a Mexican named Jose Alvarez de Toledo published *Gaceta de Texas* in 1813, the state has had a lively newspaper tradition. Texas now has about 113 daily newspapers and 345 weeklies. Newspapers with the largest circulations include the *Dallas Morning News, Dallas Times Herald,* Fort Worth *Star-Telegram,* Houston *Post,* San Antonio *Express & News,* and San Antonio *Light.* The *Texas Almanac,* a thick book containing information about Texas, has been published annually since 1857. Texas publishers also publish about 350 periodicals.

Dozens of broadcasting outlets serve the huge state. Texas has more than 70 television stations and about 570 radio stations.

**Transportation:** The vast size of Texas and its location in the center of the southern United States makes it an important transportation center. Eight interstate highways run through the state. Among them are I-40, which crosses the Panhandle; I-20, which cuts through the state from east to west; I-35, which splits the state in two as it runs north-south through Dallas-Fort Worth, Austin, and San Antonio to the Mexican border town of Laredo; and I-45, the road between Dallas and Houston. Texas contains the largest state highway system in the nation, with more than 65,000 mi. (104,605 km) of state roads.

Texas, because of its size, also leads the nation in railroad mileage. More than 13,000 mi. (20,921 km) of main-line track run through Texas. Fort Worth, Dallas, Amarillo, and Houston are the major rail centers.

The Lone Star State ranks first in aircraft departures and second in total passengers. Thirty-two Texas cities have airports with scheduled air-carrier or commuter service. The Dallas-Fort Worth Airport is one of the busiest in the United States. Other cities with large airports are Houston, San Antonio, Austin, and El Paso. Texas also is a major military air center, with fifteen air-force bases.

The Gulf of Mexico helps make Texas an important shipping center. Houston, the largest port, is one of the nation's busiest in total tonnage each year. Other major ports are Beaumont-Port Arthur, Galveston-Texas City, Corpus Christi, Brownsville, and Freeport. Although Texas is not a major river shipping center, the Intracoastal Waterway along the Sabine River handles heavy inland marine traffic.


## SOCIAL AND CULTURAL LIFE

**Museums:** Texans are known throughout the world for the pride they have in their state. That pride shows itself in hundreds of museums, most of them honoring Texas culture. Texas has about sixty-three art museums and galleries, four hundred historical museums, and twenty-seven science-and-nature museums.

It seems that nearly every town has some kind of museum honoring a local hero or a regional product. Some of these include the Old Clock Museum in Pharr, the Babe Didrickson Zaharias Memorial Museum in Beaumont, the Cattleman's Museum in Fort Worth, the Governor Hogg Shrine in Quitman, the Helmer Mercantile Lock and Tool Museum in Kermit, the National Cowgirl Hall of Fame in Hereford, the Permian Basin Petroleum Museum in Midland, and the Hal S. Smith Farm Machinery Museum in Cresson.

Texas also has museums of nationwide fame. The Amon Carter Museum of Western Art in Fort Worth enjoys a worldwide reputation. Fort Worth's Museum District also contains European and Asian art at the Kimball Art Museum and modern paintings at the Fort Worth Art Museum. The Fort Worth Museum of Science and Industry includes a planetarium and a hall of medical science as well as a hall of Texas history.

Houston boasts the Museum of Natural Science and a Museum of Fine Arts. State Fair Park in Dallas has four museums: the Museum of Natural History, the Aquarium, the Age of Steam Museum, and the Southwest Museum of Science and Technology. San Antonio's famed Alamo has a museum. The South Texas city also has the Institute of Texan Cultures, a museum that honors the state's many ethnic groups. Austin has the Texas Memorial Museum, with historical and geological exhibits. The El Paso Museum of History displays U.S. Cavalry mementoes, *charro* costumes, and other items of Southwest history.

**Libraries:** Texas's active library system includes more than 400 public libraries. During one recent year, these libraries checked out 46,407,080 books (an average of 3.3 for every Texan) and handled 5,214,689 requests for information. There are also about 150 libraries in the state's junior and senior college system. The Mirabeau B. Lamar Library at the University of Texas at Austin is the state's largest library, with 4.8 million volumes. The Lyndon Baines Johnson Library and Museum in Austin contains archives and memorabilia of the Texas son who became the country's thirty-sixth president.

**Performing Arts:** Lovers of almost any kind of music can feel at home in Texas. Black-dominated blues music predominates in East Texas. Mexican *conjuntos* playing lively German-influenced tunes prevail in South Texas. Country music can be found everywhere. Austin is famed for its clubs that offer outstanding rock and country music.

Classical music also finds a home, especially in the larger cities. Texas's more than twenty symphony orchestras include those in Houston, Dallas, San Antonio, and El Paso. The Houston Grand Opera enjoys an international reputation.

The Lone Star State claims a lively theater scene. Houstonians enjoy plays in the Nina Vance Alley Theater, which is considered one of the finest in the country. Dallas's Theatre Center offers more than 150 performances over an eight-month season. Texans also enjoy plays from many different college and university drama groups.

**Sports and Recreation:** Autumn weekends mean three things to many Texans: football, football, and more football. On Friday nights, entire towns may be found at the local high-school field to cheer the home team to victory. Saturdays belong to the colleges. Schools of all sizes compete, but some of the larger ones have become nationwide legends. Texas has eight of the nine members of the Southwest Conference: the University of Texas, Texas A & M, Texas Tech, Baylor, Rice, the University of Houston, Texas Christian University, and Southern Methodist University. The University of Arkansas is the only "outside" member of this powerful conference. On Sundays, the professional teams take over. Dallas and Fort Worth fans cheer for the Dallas Cowboys, a team so successful for so many years that it became known as "America's Team." Houston fans root for the hometown Oilers.

Other professional sports also have their followings. Baseball fans have the National League Houston Astros and American League Texas Rangers. Basketball buffs root for the San Antonio Spurs, the Houston Rockets, and the Dallas Mavericks. Rodeos, living celebrations of Texas cowboy culture, take place throughout the state.

Sportsmen find a paradise in Texas. Fishing enthusiasts can find more than 200 species in the state's many lakes, from the tiny pygmy sunfish to the 250-lb. (113-kg) alligator gar. Catfish, sunfish, bass, shiners, and walleye pike are among the other freshwater fish found in Texas. The Gulf Coast provides ample opportunities to catch marlin, tuna, and other sport fish. The numerous woodlands and fields offer hunters the chance to pursue deer, wild turkeys, antelopes, rabbits, and many other varieties of game.

Texas has two national parks. Big Bend covers about 740,000 acres (299,470 hectares) at the bend of the Rio Grande. Guadalupe Mountains National Park contains the highest peak in Texas.


**Historic Sites and Landmarks:**

*The Alamo*, in San Antonio, is the mission-turned-fortress where 189 Texans fought against thousands of Mexican soldiers for thirteen days during the War of Independence.

*Fort Concho*, in San Angelo, is among the best-preserved forts of Texas. It contains seven buildings restored to their original appearance and two others rebuilt on their original foundations.

*John F. Kennedy Memorials*, in Dallas, remind visitors that the young president was assassinated in this city in 1963. These memorials include a historical marker on the site where Kennedy was shot, a cenotaph (monument), and a memorial park.

*Mission San Jose*, in San Antonio, is considered one of the best examples of Spanish architecture in North America.

*Palmito Hill Battlefield*, near Brownsville, commemorates the last battle of the Civil War. Confederate soldiers defeated Union troops here in May 1865, unaware that Confederate General Robert E. Lee had surrendered to Union General Ulysses S. Grant at Appomattox nearly a month earlier.

**The Houston Astrodome, the world's first domed stadium**

*Republic of the Rio Grande Building,* in Laredo, serves as a history museum. Seven flags have flown over the museum: those of Spain, France, Mexico, the Republic of Texas, the Confederacy, the United States, and the unsuccessful Republic of the Rio Grande.

*San Jacinto Battleground State Historic Park,* east of Houston, marks the site of the battle in which Texas won independence from Mexico in 1836. The battleship *Texas,* which served in World War I and as flagship for the D-Day forces in World War II, is moored on the park's waterfront.

*Spindletop Museum and Lucas Gusher Monument,* in Beaumont, preserve the memory of the first big Texas gusher. The museum displays pictures and documents from Beaumont's early oil days. The monument commemorates the world's first oil boomtown.

*Texas Ranger Hall of Fame,* in Waco, honors the lawmen who helped tame the Texas frontier. It contains a replica of the original Texas Ranger fort, established in 1837.

*Washington-on-the-Brazos State Park,* near Washington, marks the spot where the Texas Declaration of Independence was signed in 1836. The Star of the Republic Museum exhibits displays concerning the time when Texas was an independent nation.

### Other Interesting Places to Visit:

*Astrodome,* in Houston, is the world's first domed stadium and one of the city's most popular attractions. Baseball's Astros and football's Oilers play there, and it is the site of the Houston Livestock Show and Rodeo.

The Governor's Mansion in Austin, built in 1856, serves as home for the Texas chief executive.

*Attwater Prairie Chicken Refuge,* in Colorado County, is a 3,400-acre (1,376-hectare) sanctuary for the once-plentiful but now rare bird.

*Big Bend National Park,* covering more than 700,000 acres (283,283 hectares) near the Rio Grande, serves as home to more than 350 bird species and 1,100 plant types. The park's land includes breathtaking canyons, a junglelike flood plain, a desert, and forest-covered mountains. Fossilized remains of prehistoric plants and animals can be seen at Persimmon Gap.

*Cave Without a Name,* near Boerne, contains dozens of stalagmites, stalactites, and unique rock formations. When the cave was opened in 1939, a contest to name it was won by a boy who wrote: "This cave is too pretty to name."

*Fighting Air Command Flying Museum,* in Denton, houses World War I and World War II aircraft in flying condition.

*Governor's Mansion,* in Austin, a white-columned mansion built in 1856, serves as home for the Texas chief executive.

*Guadalupe Mountains National Park,* about 100 miles (161 kilometers) east of El Paso, is a treasure house of wildlife and forests that contains the highest Texas peak and rugged but exciting back country.

*Institute of Texan Cultures,* in San Antonio, features exhibits of the cultures of about twenty-six ethnic groups who made Texas their home.

*Lyndon B. Johnson Space Center,* in Houston, serves as headquarters of America's manned-spaceflight program. The center displays spacecraft that have been to the moon and back, a full-scale Skylab, moon rocks, photos from Mars, and movies of space flights.

*National Mule Memorial,* in Muleshoe, is a monument to the sturdy animals that pulled covered wagons, plowed sod, and hauled freight for the first pioneers.

*Padre Island National Seashore,* on a narrow barrier island that stretches from Corpus Christi to Mexico, is an 80-mile (129-kilometer) length of sand where nature lovers can stroll in an area untouched by civilization.

*Permian Basin Petroleum Museum, Library, and Hall of Fame,* in Midland, traces the history of the area from prehistoric times to the present. It contains Indian and cowboy artifacts, early oil-industry memorabilia, a replica of a Permian Age sea, and many other models.

*River Walk (Paseo del Rio),* in San Antonio, is a pleasant landscaped path that runs for 2 miles (3 kilometers) along the San Antonio River past downtown shops, hotels, galleries, and restaurants.

*State Capitol Complex,* in the heart of Austin, occupies 46 acres (18.6 hectares). The capitol is a large building made of Texas pink granite. Office buildings and park space make up the rest of the complex.

*Water Garden,* in downtown Fort Worth, honors a substance that Texans sometimes consider more valuable than gold. The spectacular park features water fountains, channels, cascades, and pools.

## IMPORTANT DATES

c. 10,000-13,000 B.C. — The first nomadic hunters drift into land now known as Texas

c. A.D. 1400 — The Caddo Confederacy, the most-advanced of the Native American tribes in Texas, forms a civilization based on agriculture

1519 — Spanish explorer Alonso Álvarez de Piñeda maps the Texas coast

1528 — Álvar Núñez Cabeza de Vaca and other members of a shipwrecked Spanish expedition land on the Texas coast and explore the region

1541 — Spanish explorer Francisco de Coronado travels across part of western Texas in search of the famed Seven Cities of Cibola

1682 — Spaniards establish the first mission at Ysleta, near present-day El Paso

**Texas forces led by Sam Houston defeated Mexican forces led by Santa Anna in the 1836 Battle of San Jacinto, assuring Texan independence from Mexico.**

1685—French explorer René-Robert Cavelier, Sieur de La Salle, establishes a settlement at Fort Saint Louis, on the coast

1718—Spaniards found Mission San Antonio de Valero (later known as the Alamo) and a fort on the site of present-day San Antonio

1759—Comanches and allied Indian tribes rout Spaniards during a fierce battle at Spanish Fort in present-day Montague County

1813—Jose Alvarez de Toledo prints Texas's first newspaper, *Gaceta de Texas*, at Nacogdoches

1821—Mexico, including the area that is now Texas, declares its independence from Spain; the newly independent Empire of Mexico annexes Texas; the first colony of Americans settles in Texas

1836—Texas declares independence from Mexico; soldiers fend off Mexican troops for days before dying in the Alamo; forces led by Sam Houston defeat Mexicans in the Battle of San Jacinto; Texas becomes the independent Republic of Texas

1837—The United States recognizes the Republic of Texas

1839—The Republic of Texas passes a homestead exemption act, which prevents farms from being seized for payment of debts; Governor Mirabeau B. Lamar orders troops to expel many Indian tribes from Texas

A herd of longhorns is led across a stream during the days of the great cattle drives from Texas to livestock markets in Kansas.

1845 — Texas joins the Union as the twenty-eighth state

1848 — Mexico surrenders its claim to Texas after losing the Mexican War

1850 — The Compromise of 1850 sets Texas's present western boundary

1853 — Richard King buys the huge Santa Gertrudis acreage and starts the King Ranch

1859 — Texas troops destroy a Comanche settlement and kill war chief Peta Nocona

1861 — Texas secedes from the Union and joins the Confederate States of America

1865 — Union and Confederate troops, unaware that the Civil War is over, fight the Battle of Palmito Hill; federal troops enforce Reconstruction in Texas after the Civil War

1866 — Cattlemen start the first major cattle drives from Texas to livestock markets in Kansas; Lyne Taliaferro Barret drills the first producing Texas oil well, in Nacogdoches County

1870 — The U.S. government readmits Texas to the Union

1876 — Texans adopt the state's present constitution

1883 — The University of Texas opens

1891 — Governor James Hogg and the legislature establish the Texas Railroad Commission, one of the country's strongest regulatory bodies

1894 — Workers at Corsicana drill for water but instead strike oil

**The space shuttle *Atlantis* draws a crowd while on a stopover in Houston.**

1900 — Hurricane destroys Galveston and kills 6,000 people, the worst natural disaster in American history

1901 — The Lucas well at Spindletop hits a gusher, starting Texas's first major oil boom

1916 — Mexican bandit-revolutionary Pancho Villa raids the Big Bend villages of Glenn Springs and Bouquillas

1918 — Texas women gain the right to vote

1920 — The end of the Mexican Revolution marks the end of Texas-Mexico border skirmishes

1930 — Wildcatter C.M. "Dad" Joiner discovers the East Texas Oil Fields, one of the richest petroleum deposits in the world

1932 — Texan John Nance Garner is elected vice-president of the United States

1947 — About 575 persons die and 4,000 more are injured in a Texas City harbor ship explosion

1950 — The United States Supreme Court outlaws racial segregation at the University of Texas Law School

1953 — Dwight D. Eisenhower becomes the first Texas-born president; Congress restores Texas offshore tidelands to the state after a three-year battle with the federal government

1963 — An assassin kills President John F. Kennedy in Dallas and seriously injures Governor John B. Connally; Texas-born Lyndon B. Johnson is sworn in as the thirty-sixth president

1964—The Manned Space Center (now called the Lyndon Baines Johnson Space Center), headquarters for America's astronauts, opens in Houston

1965—The Houston Astrodome, the nation's first domed stadium, opens; the state legislature is reapportioned to the one man, one vote principle

1966—Katherine Anne Porter wins the Pulizter Prize in fiction for her *Collected Stories*; the poll tax is repealed

1978—Texans elect William Clements, the first Republican governor since Reconstruction

1979—A tornado rips through Wichita Falls, killing 42 people and injuring 1,740

1980—George Bush of Houston is elected vice-president of the United States

1988—George Bush is elected president of the United States; Waxahachie is selected as the future site of the superconducting super collider, the world's most powerful atom smasher

## IMPORTANT PEOPLE

**Moses Austin** (1761-1821), pioneer; entered Texas in 1820; was granted land along the Brazos River to start an Anglo farming community

**Stephen F. Austin** (1793-1836), pioneer; known as the "Father of Texas"; governed settlers of the Anglo colony started by his father, Moses; led movement for Texas independence; named first secretary of state of the Republic of Texas

**Gene Autry** (1907-    ), born in Tioga; singer, actor, businessman; starred in dozens of cowboy movies; his recording of "Rudolph the Red-Nosed Reindeer" became one of the best-selling songs of all time; owner of baseball's American League California Angels

**Eugene C. Barker** (1874-1956), born near Riverside; historian; University of Texas professor who was instrumental in documenting the career of Stephen F. Austin and the Texas struggle for independence

**Sammy "Slingin' Sammy" Baugh** (1914-    ), born in Temple; professional football player; Texas football legend who was a Texas Christian University and Washington Redskins star quarterback

**GENE AUTRY**

**SAMMY BAUGH**

**EARL CAMPBELL**

**HENRY CISNEROS**

**JOHN CONNALLY**

**DWIGHT D. EISENHOWER**

**Gail Borden, Jr.** (1801-1874), inventor and journalist; invented evaporated milk; published newspapers and pamphlets promoting the Republic of Texas

**James Bowie** (1796?-1836), soldier; invented the Bowie knife; died at the Battle of the Alamo

**George Herbert Walker Bush** (1924-    ), forty-first president of the United States (1989-    ); Zapata Petroleum Corp. executive, Houston (1953-66); U.S. congressman (1967-71); Central Intelligence Agency director (1976-77); vice-president of U.S. (1981-89)

**Earl Christian Campbell** (1955-    ), born in Tyler; professional football player; running back with the University of Texas and the Houston Oilers; won Heisman Trophy (1977)

**Carlos E. Castaneda** (1896-1958), writer, historian; author of a dozen books and numerous articles dealing with Texas and Mexican border history

**Henry G. Cisneros** (1947-    ), born in San Antonio; educator, politician; mayor of San Antonio (1981-    ); national Hispanic leader

**John Bowden Connally** (1917-    ), born near Floresville; politician; U.S. secretary of the navy (1961); governor (1963-69); wounded during attack that killed President John F. Kennedy; U.S. secretary of the treasury (1971-72)

**Thomas Connally** (1877-1963), born near Hewitt; politician; U.S. congressman (1917-29); U.S. senator (1929-53); sponsored the Connally Resolution, which made the U.S. a leading participant in the United Nations

**Denton Arthur Cooley** (1920-    ), born in Houston; surgeon; open-heart surgery pioneer

**David (Davy) Crockett** (1786-1836), frontiersman; hero of the Battle of the Alamo

**J. Frank Dobie** (1888-1964), born in Live Oak County; writer; reorganized Texas Folklore Society; wrote *A Vaquero in the Brush Country* and *Coronado's Children*

**Clara Driscoll** (1881-1945), born in St. Mary's; historic preservationist, politician; led fight to preserve the Alamo; for sixteen years was a Democratic national committeewoman

**John C. Duval** (1819-1897), writer; called the Father of Texas Literature; wrote *The Adventures of Big Foot Wallace* and *Early Times in Texas*

**Dwight David Eisenhower** (1890-1969), born in Denison; thirty-fourth president of the United States (1953-61); general who commanded allied troops in Europe during World War II; orchestrated D-Day invasion; established Air Force Academy during presidency

**James Farmer** (1920-    ), born in Marshall; civil-rights leader; founder of the Congress of Racial Equality (CORE)

**Freddy Fender** (1937-    ), born Baldomar Huerta in San Benito; singer; recorded "Before the Next Teardrop Falls"

**Miriam A. "Ma" Ferguson** (1875-1961), born in Bell County; politician; governor of Texas (1925-27, 1933-35); aided farmers and workers; opposed the Ku Klux Klan

**John Nance Garner** (1868-1967), born near Uvalde; politician; Speaker of the House of Representatives (1931-33); U.S. vice-president (1933-41)

**Henry B. Gonzalez** (1916-    ), born in San Antonio; U.S. congressman (1961-    ); senior Mexican American member of the House of Representatives

**Larry Hagman** (1931-    ), born in Weatherford; actor; known throughout the world for his role as J.R. Ewing in television show *Dallas*

**O. Henry**, pen name of William Sydney Porter (1862-1910), writer; famed for short stories that end with an unexpected twist; wrote *The Gift of the Magi* and *The Ransom of Red Chief*

**Oveta Culp Hobby** (1905-    ), born in Killeen; newspaper publisher and social reformer; published Houston *Post*; first director, Women's Army Corps; first secretary of health, education, and welfare (1953-55)

**Ben Hogan** (1912-    ), born in Dublin; professional golfer; won two Masters, four U.S. Opens, two PGAs, and one British Open championship; elected to PGA Hall of Fame (1953)

**Ima Hogg** (1882-1975), born in Mineola; philanthropist; helped found Houston Symphony Orchestra (1913); founded Houston Child Guidance Clinic

**James Stephen Hogg** (1851-1906), born near Rusk; politician; first Texas-born governor (1891-95); one of the most progressive and respected governors in Texas history

**Buddy Holly** (1936-1959), born in Lubbock; musician and songwriter; one of the major early rock-and-roll artists; his music influenced the Rolling Stones and the Beatles; recorded "That'll Be the Day" and "Peggy Sue"

**Rogers Hornsby** (1896-1963), born in Winters; professional baseball player; second baseman with the St. Louis Cardinals and the Chicago Cubs; considered by many the best right-handed batter in history

**Samuel (Sam) Houston** (1793-1863), soldier, politician; leader of the Battle of San Jacinto; first president of the Republic of Texas (1836-38, 1841-44); U.S. senator (1846-49); governor (1859-61)

**JAMES FARMER**

**OVETA CULP HOBBY**

**BUDDY HOLLY**

**ROGERS HORNSBY**

**HOWARD HUGHES**

**JACK JOHNSON**

**SCOTT JOPLIN**

**RICHARD KING**

**Howard Robard Hughes** (1905-1976), born in Houston; industrialist, aviator; reclusive millionaire; inventor of the Spruce Goose wooden airplane; noted film producer

**Haroldson Lafayette (H.L.) Hunt** (1889-1974), businessman; petroleum magnate; one of the richest men in the world, his income was estimated at $1 million per week; known for his ultra-conservative views

**Waylon Jennings** (1937-      ), born in Littlefield; musician; famed ''outlaw'' country singer who often sang with Willie Nelson; recorded ''Good Hearted Woman'' and ''Luckenbach, Texas''

**Arthur ''Jack'' Johnson** (1878-1946), born in Galveston; professional boxer; became first heavyweight boxing champion (1908)

**Lyndon Baines Johnson** (1908-1972), born near Stonewall; thirty-sixth president of the United States (1963-69); vice-president of U.S. (1961-63); as president, passed historic civil-rights and War on Poverty legislation; responsible for escalation of Vietnam War

**Anson Jones** (1798-1858), politician; secretary of state, Republic of Texas (1841); president of Republic of Texas (1844-46); laid groundwork for annexation of Texas by U.S.

**Jesse Holman Jones** (1874-1956), financier, public official; played key role in creation of Houston Ship Channel and Port of Houston; U.S. secretary of commerce (1940-45)

**Janis Joplin** (1938-1970), born in Port Arthur; singer; considered by many to be the finest white blues singer; recorded ''Me and Bobbie McGee''

**Scott Joplin** (1868-1917), born in Texarkana; musician; considered the originator of ragtime music; wrote more than five hundred pieces of music, including a ballet and two operas

**Barbara C. Jordan** (1936-      ), born in Houston; lawyer, politician; first black woman from a southern state to be elected to U.S. House of Representatives (1973-79); distinguished by her eloquence during the Nixon impeachment hearings and the 1976 Democratic National Convention

**Richard King** (1825-1885), rancher, businessman; founded the King Ranch in southern Texas, at his death the largest in the U.S.

**Mirabeau Buonaparte Lamar** (1798-1859), politician; second president of the Republic of Texas (1838-41); organized the Texas public school system; ordered Indians removed from Texas lands

**Thomas Wade (Tom) Landry** (1924-      ), born in Mission; professional football coach; first coach of the Dallas cowboys (1960-89); led the team to five Super Bowls and two world championships

**Stanley Marcus** (1905-      ), born in Dallas; businessman; co-founder of the world-famous Neiman-Marcus stores

**Mary Martin** (1913-    ), born in Weatherford; singer, actress; best known for her role as Peter Pan

**Audie Murphy** (1924-1971), born in Kingston; soldier, actor; most decorated U.S. World War II hero; later starred in many films

**Jose Antonio Navarro** (1795-1871), born in San Antonio; politician; one of the drafters of the Republic of Texas constitution; helped write the first state constitution

**Willie Nelson** (1933-    ), born in Abbott; musician; country-and-western singer best known for his wide variety of musical styles; recorded "Blue Skies," "Whiskey River," and "Georgia on My Mind"

**Elisabet Ney** (1833-1907), settled in Texas; sculptor, feminist; helped found the Texas Fine Arts Association

**Chester William Nimitz** (1885-1966), born in Fredericksburg; naval officer; commander-in-chief U.S. Pacific fleet during World War II

**Katherine Anne Porter** (1890-1980), born in Indian Creek; writer; won 1966 Pulitzer Prize in literature for *Collected Stories*; wrote *Ship of Fools* (1962)

**Samuel Taliaferro (Sam) Rayburn** (1882-1961), lived in Texas from 1887; politician; U.S. congressman (1913-61); Speaker of the House of Representatives (1940-46, 1949-53, 1955-61); encouraged establishment of the United Nations; considered one of the nation's best and most talented legislators

**Thomas Jefferson Rusk** (1803-1857), lived in Texas from 1835; public official; fought alongside Sam Houston at San Jacinto; chief justice of Texas Supreme Court; president of 1845 constitutional convention; worked to improve early Texas transportation and communication

**Nolan Ryan** (1947-    ), born in Refugio; professional baseball player, pitcher; all-time strike-out king; threw a record five no-hit games; led Houston Astros to Western Division titles in 1980 and 1986

**William Lee "Willie" Shoemaker** (1931-    ), born in Fabens; professional jockey; rode four Kentucky Derby, one Preakness, and five Belmont Stakes winners

**Ashbel Smith** (1805-1886), physician, politician; surgeon general of the Republic of Texas (1857); Texas secretary of state (1845)

**Tristam (Tris) Speaker** (1888-1958), born in Hubbard; professional baseball player; considered by many to be baseball's greatest center fielder

**Roger Thomas Staubach** (1942-    ), professional football player; considered one of the game's greatest passers; won Heisman Trophy (1963); led Dallas Cowboys to four Super Bowls and two Super Bowl championships; named to National Football League Hall of Fame (1985)

**MARY MARTIN**

**AUDIE MURPHY**

**CHESTER W. NIMITZ**

**SAM RAYBURN**

**BABE D. ZAHARIAS**

**John Goodwin Tower** (1925-      ), born in Houston; politician; U.S. senator (1961-85); known as one of the most articulate conservative voices in the Senate; chairman of the Senate Armed Services Committee

**William Barret Travis** (1809-1836); commanded Texas forces at the Alamo

**James Wright** (1922-      ), born in Fort Worth; politician; U.S. congressman (1954-    ); Speaker of the House of Representatives (1987-    )

**Mildred "Babe" Didrikson Zaharias** (1913-1956), born in Port Arthur; athlete; All-American basketball player (1930); won two Olympic track-and-field gold medals (1932); leading woman golfer in 1940s and early 1950s; greatest female athlete of the twentieth century; gained worldwide admiration for her fight against cancer

## GOVERNORS

| | | | |
|---|---|---|---|
| J. Pinckney Henderson | 1846-1847 | Oscar B. Colquitt | 1911-1915 |
| George T. Wood | 1847-1849 | James E. Ferguson | 1915-1917 |
| P. Hansborough Bell | 1849-1853 | William P. Hobby | 1917-1921 |
| J.W. Henderson | 1853 | Pat M. Neff | 1921-1925 |
| Elisha M. Pease | 1853-1857 | Miriam A. Ferguson | 1925-1927 |
| Hardin R. Runnels | 1857-1859 | Dan Moody | 1927-1931 |
| Sam Houston | 1859-1861 | Ross Sterling | 1931-1933 |
| Edward Clark | 1861 | Miriam A. Ferguson | 1933-1935 |
| Francis R. Lubbock | 1861-1863 | James V. Allred | 1935-1939 |
| Pendleton Murrah | 1863-1865 | W. Lee O'Daniel | 1939-1941 |
| Andrew J. Hamilton | 1865-1866 | Coke R. Stevenson | 1941-1947 |
| James W. Throckmorton | 1866-1867 | Beauford H. Jester | 1947-1949 |
| Elisha M. Pease | 1867-1869 | Allan Shivers | 1949-1957 |
| Edmund J. Davis | 1870-1874 | Price Daniel | 1957-1963 |
| Richard Coke | 1874-1876 | John B. Connally | 1963-1969 |
| Richard B. Hubbard | 1876-1879 | Preston Smith | 1969-1973 |
| Oran M. Roberts | 1879-1883 | Dolph Briscoe | 1973-1979 |
| John Ireland | 1883-1887 | William P. Clements | 1979-1983 |
| Lawrence S. Ross | 1887-1891 | Mark White | 1983-1987 |
| James S. Hogg | 1891-1895 | William P. Clements | 1987- |
| Charles A. Culberson | 1895-1899 | | |
| Joseph D. Sayers | 1899-1903 | | |
| S.W.T. Lanham | 1903-1907 | | |
| Thomas M. Campbell | 1907-1911 | | |

## Topography

# MAP KEY

| Place | Ref | | Place | Ref |
|---|---|---|---|---|
| Abilene | C3 | | Concho (river) | D2,3 |
| Alamito Creek (creek) | o,p12,13 | | Cooper | C5 |
| Alamo | F3 | | Copperas | D3 |
| Alanreed | B2 | | Cornudas | o12 |
| Alba | C5 | | Corpus Christi | F4 |
| Allamoore | o12 | | Corpus Christi Naval Air Station | F4 |
| Alta Loma | r14 | | Corsicana | C4 |
| Amarillo | B2 | | Cove | D4;r15 |
| Amistad Recreation Area | E2 | | Coyanosa Draw (shallow gully) | D1 |
| Apache Mountains (mountains) | o12 | | Cross | D4 |
| Apple Springs | D5 | | Cuero | E4 |
| Aransas Bay (bay) | E4 | | Cypress | r14 |
| Arlington | n9 | | Cypress Creek (creek) | q,r14 |
| Arlington Lake (lake) | n9 | | Dalhart | A1 |
| Austin | D4 | | Dallas | C4;n10 |
| Baffins Bay (bay) | F4 | | Dallas Naval Air Station | n10 |
| Bardwell Lake (lake) | D4 | | Davis Mountains (mountains) | o12,13 |
| Batson | D5 | | Dawn | B1 |
| Baytown | E5;r14,15 | | Delaware Mountains (mountains) | o12 |
| Beaumont | D5 | | Delmita | F3 |
| Belton Lake (lake) | D4 | | Denton | C4 |
| Ben Bolt | F3 | | Devils (river) | D,E2 |
| Benbrook Lake (lake) | n9 | | Dilley | E3 |
| Bergstrom Air Force Base | D4 | | Dinero | E4 |
| Bessmay | D6 | | Double Bayou | r15 |
| Best | D2 | | Doucetta | D5 |
| Big Bend National Park | E1;p13 | | Dripping Springs | D3 |
| Big Lake | D2 | | Dundee | C3 |
| Bigfoot | E3 | | Dunn | C2 |
| Blooming Grove | C4 | | Dyess Air Force Base | C3 |
| Bluff Dale | C3,4 | | Eagle Lake | E4 |
| Boerne | E3;h7 | | Eagle Mountain (mountain) | o12 |
| Boyce | n10 | | Eagle Mountain Lake (lake) | m,n9 |
| Boys Ranch | B1 | | Eagle Pass | E2 |
| Bradshaw | C3 | | East Bay | r15 |
| Brady Mountains (mountains) | D3 | | East Fork (fork, Trinity River) | n10 |
| Brazos (river) | D,E4,5;r,s14 | | Edwards Plateau (plateau) | D2,3 |
| Bronco | C1 | | El Indio | E2 |
| Bronson | D5,6 | | El Paso | o11 |
| Brooks Air Force Base | k7 | | Eldorado | D2 |
| Brownsville | G4 | | Electra | C3 |
| Buffalo Lake (lake) | B1 | | Elm Fork (fork, Trinity River) | m,n10 |
| Buna | D6 | | Emory Peak (peak) | E1;p13 |
| Burkburnett | B3 | | Encinal | E3 |
| Burkett | C,D3 | | Encino | F3 |
| Burkeville | D6 | | Enterprise | D5 |
| Burnet | D3 | | Esta (mountains) | C1 |
| Caddo | C3 | | Falcon | F3 |
| Caddo Lake (lake) | C5 | | Fannin | E4 |
| Camden | D5 | | Fentress | h8 |
| Camp Ruby | D5 | | Flomot | B2 |
| Camp San Saba | D3 | | Florey | C1 |
| Canadian (river) | B1,2 | | Forest | D5 |
| Candelaria | o12 | | Forsan | C2 |
| Canton | C5 | | Fort Davis | o13 |
| Cany Creek (creek) | r,s14 | | Fort Hancock | o12 |
| Canyon | B2 | | Fort Hood | D4 |
| Canyon Lake (lake) | E3;h7 | | Fort Sam Houston | k7 |
| Capote Hills | k7,8 | | Fort Worth | C4;n9 |
| Capote Knob (knob) | k8 | | Fredericksburg | D3 |
| Carlsbad | D2 | | Freeport | E5;s14 |
| Carlton | D3 | | Frio (river) | E3 |
| Carmine | D4 | | Friona | B1 |
| Carrizo Creek (creek) | A,B1 | | Galveston | E5;r15 |
| Carswell Air Force Base | n9 | | Galveston Bay (bay) | E5;r15 |
| Carta Valley | E2 | | Galveston Island (island) | E5;r14,15 |
| Casa Piedra | p12 | | Garciasville | F3 |
| Cathedral Mountain (mountain) | o13 | | Garland | n10 |
| Cedar Creek | D4 | | Garza-Little Elm Reservoir (reservoir) | C4;m9,10 |
| Cedar Creek Reservoir (reservoir) | C4,5 | | Georgetown | D4 |
| Cedar Lake | E5 | | Glass Mountains (mountains) | D1;o13 |
| Cerro Alto Mountain (mountain) | o12 | | Glazier | A,B2 |
| Champion Creek Reservoir (reservoir) | C2 | | Goldsmith | D1 |
| Chapman Ranch | F4 | | Goliad | E4 |
| Chase Field Naval Air Station | E4 | | Gonzales | E4 |
| Cherokee | D3 | | Goodfellow Air Force Base | D2 |
| Cheyenne | D1 | | Goodnight | B2 |
| Chicota | C5 | | Grand Prairie | n10 |
| Childress | B2 | | Grapevine | C4;n9 |
| Chinati Peak (peak) | p12 | | Grapevine Lake | m,n9 |
| Chisos Mountains (mountains) | E1;p13 | | Gross Plains | C3 |
| Chocolate Bayou | r14 | | Grow | C2 |
| Christine | E3 | | Guadalupe (river) | h7,8;k8 |
| Christoval | D2 | | Guadalupe Mountains National Park | o12 |
| Cibolo Creek (creek) | h,k7 | | Guadalupe Peak (peak) | o12 |
| Cistern | E4 | | Guerra | F3 |
| Clarendon | B2 | | Gulf of Mexico (gulf) | E,F4,5,6;r,s14,15 |
| Clyde | C3 | | Gustine | D3 |
| Coldwater Creek (creek) | A1,2 | | Happy | B2 |
| College Station | D4 | | Harlingen | F4 |
| Colorado (river) | D2,3,4;E4,5 | | Hedley | B2 |
| Coltexo | B2 | | | |
| Concepcion | F3 | | | |

| Place | Ref | | Place | Ref |
|---|---|---|---|---|
| Helotes | h7 | | Port Arthur | E6 |
| Henderson | C5 | | Port Bolivar | E5;r15 |
| Hereford | B1 | | Port Isabel | F4 |
| Hitchland | A2 | | Port Lavaca | E4 |
| Houston | E5;r14 | | Port O'Connor | E4 |
| Houston Intercontinental Airport | r14 | | Porter | D5 |
| Hubbard Creek Reservoir (reservoir) | C3 | | Prade Ranch | E3 |
| Hueco Mountains (mountains) | o11,12 | | Proctor Lake (lake) | C,D3 |
| Hunter | E3;h7 | | Pumpville | E2 |
| Hye | D3 | | Quemado | E2 |
| Imperial | D1 | | Quitague | B2 |
| Indian Gap | D3 | | Quitman Mountains (mountains) | o12 |
| Indian Reservation (Indian reservation) | D5 | | Randolph Air Force Base | h7 |
| Inez | E4 | | Realitos | F3 |
| Intracostal Waterway | E5 | | Red (river) | B,C2,3,4,5 |
| Ira | C2 | | Red Bluff Reservoir (reservoir) | o13 |
| Irving | n10 | | Reese Air Force Base | C1 |
| Jermyn | C3 | | Richland Springs | D3 |
| Johnson City | D3 | | Riesel | D4 |
| Johntown | C5 | | Ringgold | C4 |
| Jolly | C3 | | Rio Grande (river) | E1,2;F3,4;G4; o11,12;p12,13 |
| Karnes City | E4 | | Riviera | F4 |
| Kelly Air Force Base | k7 | | Roaring Springs | C2 |
| Kerrville | D,E3 | | Rockport | E,F4 |
| Kilgore | C5 | | Rockwall | C4;n10 |
| Killeen | D4 | | Rockwood | D3 |
| Kingsville Naval Air Station | F4 | | Roma | F3 |
| Kirkland | B2 | | Roosevelt | D2 |
| Klondike | C5 | | Round Mountain | D3 |
| Knickerbocker | D2 | | Royalty | D1 |
| Knott | C2 | | Rusk | D5 |
| Laguna Madre (lagoon) | F4 | | Sabine (river) | D,E6 |
| Lake Brownwood (lake) | D3 | | Sabine Pass | E6 |
| Lake Colorado City (lake) | C2 | | Sacul | D5 |
| Lake Graham (lake) | C3 | | Salmon Peak (peak) | E2 |
| Lake Houston (lake) | q,r14 | | Salt Basin (basin) | o12 |
| Lake J. B. Thomas (lake) | C2 | | Sam Rayburn Reservoir (reservoir) | D5 |
| Lake Kemp (lake) | C3 | | San Angelo | D2 |
| Lake Kickapoo (lake) | C3 | | San Antonio | E3;k7 |
| Lake Meredith (lake) | B2 | | San Antonio (river) | k7 |
| Lake Meredith National Recreational Area | B2 | | San Antonio Bay (bay) | E4 |
| Lake Mexia (lake) | D4 | | San Jacinto (river) | r14 |
| Lake Nasworthy (lake) | D2 | | San Jose Island (island) | E,F4 |
| Lake O' the Pines (lake) | C5 | | San Luis Pass (pass) | r14 |
| Lake Palestine (lake) | C5 | | San Marcos | E4;h8 |
| Lake Pat Cleburn (lake) | C4 | | San Marcos (river) | h8 |
| Lake Stamford (lake) | C3 | | Santiago Mountains (mountains) | D,E1;o,p13 |
| Lake Tawakoni (lake) | C4,5 | | Santiago Peak (peak) | E1;p13 |
| Lake Texarkana (lake) | C5 | | Santo | C3 |
| Lake Tyler (lake) | C5 | | Saragosa | D1;o13 |
| Lakeview | B2 | | Saspamco | k7 |
| Laredo | F3 | | Seminole | C1 |
| Lariat | B1 | | Seven Sisters | E,F3 |
| Latexo | D5 | | Sheffield | D2 |
| Lavon Lake (lake) | m10 | | Shepherd Air Force Base | C3 |
| Lawn | C3 | | Sherman | C4 |
| Lela Lake | B2 | | Sierra Blanco (mountain) | o12 |
| Lenorah | C2 | | Sierra Diablo (mountains) | o12 |
| Lewisville | C4;m10 | | Sierra Vieja Mountains (mountains) | o12 |
| Lillian | n9 | | Sinton | E4 |
| Linn | F3 | | Smiley | E4;k8 |
| Little Cypress Creek (creek) | q,r14 | | Somerville Lake (lake) | D4 |
| Livermore Peak (peak) | o12 | | Spanish Fort | C4 |
| Liverpool | r14 | | Spring | q14 |
| Llano (mountains) | C1 | | Spring Branch | h7 |
| Llano (river) | D2,3 | | Stamford | C3 |
| Lobo | o12 | | Stillhouse Hollow Reservoir (reservoir) | D4 |
| Lockland Air Force Base | k7 | | Stockton Plateau (plateau) | D1,2 |
| Longview | C5 | | Sunset | C3 |
| Los Ebanos | F3 | | Sweet Home | E4 |
| Lubbock | C2 | | Swenson | C2 |
| Lufkin | D5 | | Terlingua | p13 |
| Luling | E4;h8 | | Terlingua Creek (creek) | o,p13 |
| Lyndon B. Johnson Space Center | r14 | | Terrell Hills | k7 |
| Magic City | B2 | | Texarkana | C5 |
| Marshall | C5 | | Texas City | E5;r15 |
| Mason | D3 | | Texhoma | A2 |
| Matagorda | E5 | | Texon | D2 |
| Matagorda Bay (bay) | E4,5 | | Thornton | D4 |
| Matagorda Island (island) | E4 | | Toledo Bend Reservoir (reservoir) | C,D5,6 |
| Matagorda Peninsula (peninsula) | E4,5 | | Trent | C2 |
| McAllen | F3 | | Trinity (river) | C4,D4,5,E5 |
| McNeil | D4 | | Turkey | B2 |
| Meadow | C1 | | Tuscola | C3 |
| Mendota | B2 | | Twin Buttes Reservoir (reservoir) | D2 |
| Mesquite | n10 | | Tyler | C5 |
| Mexia | D4 | | University Park | n10 |
| Midland | D1 | | Utopia | E3 |
| Millersview | D3 | | Valentine | o12 |
| Mission | F3 | | Valley Spring | D3 |
| Mobeetie | B2 | | Valley View | C4 |
| Mount Pleasant | C5 | | Vanderpool | E3 |
| Mountain Home | D3 | | Vealmoor | C2 |
| Mustang Draw (gully) | C1,2 | | Vera | C3 |
| Nacogdoches | D5 | | Vesey | C5 |
| Navarro Mills Lake (lake) | D4 | | Victoria | E4 |
| New Braunfels | E3;h7 | | Voca | D3 |
| Newark | n9 | | Von Ormy | k7 |
| North Fork (fork, Red River) | B2 | | Waco | D4 |
| North Zulch | D4 | | Waco Lake (lake) | D4 |
| Northfield | B2 | | Water Valley | D2 |
| Norton | D2 | | Wayside | B2 |
| Nueces (river) | E3 | | Webb | F3 |
| Oakalla | D4 | | Webb Air Force Base | C2 |
| Odessa | D1 | | Welch | C1 |
| Oilton | F3 | | Wellborn | D4 |
| Orange | D6 | | Wellman | C1 |
| Ozona | D2 | | West Bay (bay) | r14,15 |
| Padre Island (island) | F4 | | West Fork (fork, Trinity River) | n9 |
| Padre Island National Seashore | F4 | | Westhoff | E4 |
| Palo Duro Canyon (canyon) | B2 | | White (river) | B,C2 |
| Palodura | B2 | | Whiteflat | B2 |
| Pampa | B2 | | Whitt | C3,4 |
| Pasadena | r14 | | Wichita Falls | C3 |
| Pawnee | E4 | | Wiildorado | B1 |
| Pease (river) | B2,3 | | Willow City | D3 |
| Pecos (river) | D1,2;E2;o13 | | Wolf Creek (creek) | A2 |
| Penitas | F3 | | Wortham | D4 |
| Perryton | A2 | | Yoakum | E4 |
| Plainview | B2 | | Zavalla | D5 |
| Pontotoc | D3 | | Zephyr | D3 |
| Poolville | C4 | | | |

Lambert Conformal Conic Projection

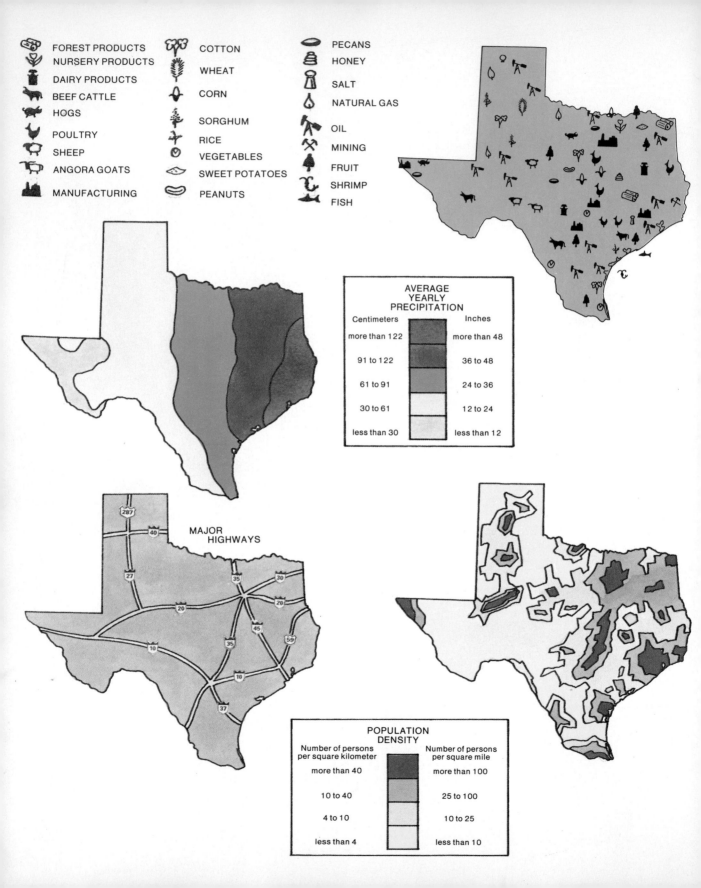

FOREST PRODUCTS
NURSERY PRODUCTS
DAIRY PRODUCTS
BEEF CATTLE
HOGS
POULTRY
SHEEP
ANGORA GOATS
MANUFACTURING

COTTON
WHEAT
CORN
SORGHUM
RICE
VEGETABLES
SWEET POTATOES
PEANUTS

PECANS
HONEY
SALT
NATURAL GAS
OIL
MINING
FRUIT
SHRIMP
FISH

AVERAGE
YEARLY
PRECIPITATION

Centimeters          Inches

more than 122        more than 48

91 to 122            36 to 48

61 to 91             24 to 36

30 to 61             12 to 24

less than 30         less than 12

MAJOR
HIGHWAYS

POPULATION
DENSITY

Number of persons          Number of persons
per square kilometer        per square mile

more than 40               more than 100

10 to 40                   25 to 100

4 to 10                    10 to 25

less than 4                less than 10

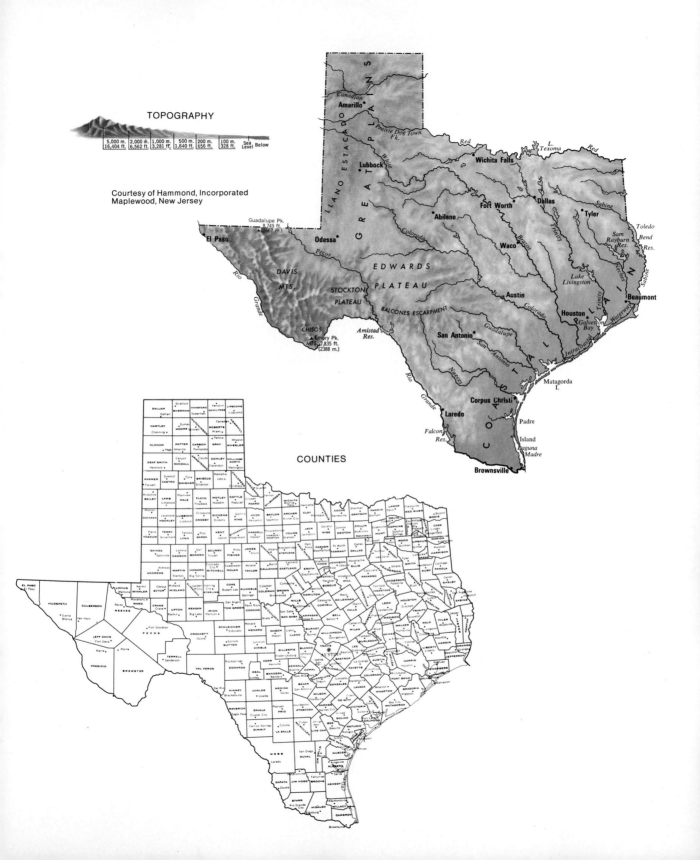

## TOPOGRAPHY

| 5,000 m. | 2,000 m. | 1,000 m. | 500 m. | 200 m. | 100 m. | Sea |
|---|---|---|---|---|---|---|
| 16,404 ft. | 6,562 ft. | 3,281 ft. | 1,640 ft. | 656 ft. | 328 ft. | Level Below |

Courtesy of Hammond, Incorporated
Maplewood, New Jersey

## COUNTIES

Texas longhorn cattle, once the mainstays of Texas herds, have returned to favor in recent years because of the leanness of their meat.

# INDEX

**Page numbers that appear in boldface type indicate illustrations**

**Lush East Texas farmland**

**Picture Identifications**

**Front Cover:** Dallas at night
**Back Cover:** Sunrise over the Rio Grande and the Chisos Mountains, Big Bend National Park
**Pages 2-3:** Sierra del Carmen, Big Bend National Park
**Page 6:** A cowboy during roundup at a cattle and sheep ranch near San Angelo
**Pages 8-9:** A view of the barren Chisos Mountains from the Sotol Vista overlook, Big Bend National Park
**Pages 20-21:** A montage of Texas residents
**Page 28:** René-Robert Cavelier, Sieur de La Salle, landing on the coast of the Gulf of Mexico
**Pages 38-39:** *The Fall of the Alamo,* by Robert Jenkins Onderdonk (1852-1917)
**Page 52:** *In a Stampede,* an 1888 illustration by Frederic Remington
**Page 62:** A NASA rocket exhibit at the Johnson Space Center, Houston
**Pages 70-71:** The capitol building, Austin
**Pages 82-83:** A Texas *Cinco de Mayo* Festival
**Pages 92-93:** The Dallas skyline at dusk
**Page 109:** Montage showing the state flag, state tree (pecan), state flower (bluebonnet), state bird (mockingbird), state grass (sideoats grama), and state gem (topaz)

## About the Author

R. Conrad Stein was born and grew up in Chicago. He received a degree in history from the University of Illinois and later studied at the University of Guanajuato in Mexico. Mr. Stein now lives in Chicago with his wife and their daughter Janna. He is the author of many books written for young readers. Mr. Stein has traveled in Texas, and for many years has read Texas lore. The author wishes especially to thank the staff of the Institute of Texan Cultures in San Antonio for their help in preparing this book.

## Picture Acknowledgments

**H. Armstrong Roberts:** © Camerique: Front cover
**Tom Stack & Associates:** © Tom Algire Photography: Back cover, Pages 105 (left), 106; © Jeff Foott: Page 17 (top left); © Jim McNee: Page 77 (right); © Matt Bradley: Page 99 (left)
**Root Resources:** © Jan Bannan: Pages 2-3; © Garry D. McMichael: Pages 12, 13 (top right), 27 (right), 78 (left), 104; © Laurence Parent: Pages 13 (top left), 74 (right); © Charlene Faris: Pages 24 (left), 97; © Bill Barksdale: Page 77 (bottom left); © V. Redin: Page 87 (left); © James Blank: Pages 92-93
**Odyssey Productions:** © Walter Frerck: Pages 4, 11 (left), 19, 20 (bottom right), 78 (right), 80 (left), 88; © Robert Frerck: Pages 6, 21 (top and middle), 76 (top and bottom right)
**Shostal Associates:** Pages 13 (bottom right), 14, 18, 77 (top left), 113; © Bob Glander: Pages 5, 62, 70-71, 121; © W.D. Murphy: Pages 33 (right), 102, 108 (background picture); © Lou Witt: Page 108 (top left); © W. Plaster: Page 141
**Journalism Services:** © Dave Brown: Pages 8-9, 115; © Oscar Williams: Page 13 (middle left)
**Photri:** Pages 16 (top middle), 17 (bottom left), 69 (right), 95, 108 (middle right); © M. Long: Pages 11 (right), 75 (right), 117; © J. Novak: Page 16 (bottom left); © Leonard Lee Rue: Pages 17 (bottom middle), 108 (bottom left); © Blakesley: Page 17 (bottom right); © Scott Berner: Pages 34, 80 (right), 99 (right), 100, 103, 107, 114
**SuperStock International:** Pages 96 (right), 98; © E. Ludwig: Page 13 (bottom left)
**EKM-Nepenthe:** Page 126; © R.L. Potts: Page 16 (top left)
© **Jerry Hennen:** Page 16 (top right)
© **Joan Dunlop:** Pages 16 (bottom right), 21 (middle right), 89 (right), 108 (bottom right)
**Photo Options:** © Steve Price: Pages 17 (top right), 138; © David Dobbs: Page 75 (left)
**TSW-Click/Chicago:** © Robert E. Daemmrich: Pages 20 (bottom left, middle left, top left, top right), 21 (middle left, bottom right), 82-83, 87 (right), 90 (top and bottom left); © Bob Thomason: Page 24 (right); © Brian Seed: Page 27 (left); © Steve Elmore: Page 105 (right)
**Marilyn Gartman Agency:** © Eric Futran Photography: Page 21 (bottom left); © Ellis Herwig: Page 96 (left); © Audrey Gibson: Page 122
**The Granger Collection:** Pages 28, 31, 33 (left), 41 (right), 44 (left and middle), 45 (right), 52, 57, 59, 125, 130 (Joplin and King)
**Courtesy of the Texas Memorial Museum:** Page 30
**Courtesy of the Texas Memorial Museum, Mrs. Russell H. Fish, III:** Page 47
**Nettie Lee Benson Collection, General Libraries, University of Texas at Austin:** Page 36
**National Museum of American Art, Smithsonian Institution, Gift of Mrs. Joseph Harrison, Jr.:** Page 37
**Friends of the Governor's Mansion:** Pages 38-39
**Courtesy Daughters of the Republic of Texas Library, San Antonio:** Page 41
**Historical Pictures Service, Inc., Chicago:** Pages 43, 44 (right), 45 (left), 130 (Johnson), 131 (Rayburn)
**Western History Collections, University of Oklahoma Library:** Page 48
**Austin History Center, Austin Public Library:** Page 51
**The Erwin E. Smith Collection of the Library of Congress on deposit at the Amon Carter Museum:** Page 55 (all three pictures)
**The Bettmann Archive:** Pages 56 (both pictures), 60, 64, 129 (Hobby and Hornsby)
**UPI/Bettmann Newsphotos:** Page 128 (Cisneros), 129 (Farmer and Holly), 131 (Nimitz)
**AP/Wide World Photos, Inc.:** Pages 67, 69, 127 (both pictures), 128 (Campbell and Connally), 130 (top), 131 (Martin and Murphy), 132
**Tourism Division, TX Dept. of Commerce:** photo by Richard Reynolds: Page 74 (left); photo by Michael Murphy: Page 89 (left)
**Cameramann International Ltd.:** Pages 76 (left), 90 (right)
**Austin History Center, Austin Public Library, Chalberg Collection:** Page 85 (left)
**Courtesy of the Artist, Luis Jimenez:** Page 85 (right)
**Third Coast Stock Source:** © Darryl Baird: Page 112
**R.W. Norton Art Gallery:** Page 124
**U.S. Bureau of Engraving and Printing:** Page 128 (bottom)
**Len W. Meents:** Maps on pages 95, 97, 98, 100, 103, 104, 136
**Courtesy Flag Research Center, Winchester, Massachusetts 01890:** Flag on page 108